Legal Fictions

Legal
Fictions

Lon L. Fuller

Stanford University Press
Stanford, California

Originally published as three articles in the
Illinois Law Review, XXV (1930–31)
First published in book form in 1967

Stanford University Press
Stanford, California
Printed in the United States of America
Cloth ISBN 0-8047-0327-2
Paper ISBN 0-8047-0328-0
Original edition 1967
Last figure below indicates year of this printing:
86 85 84 83 82 81 80 79 78 77

Contents

Introduction

The three chapters of this book originally appeared in 1930 and 1931 as a series of articles in the *Illinois Law Review* (Vol. 25, nos. 4, 5, and 6). Thus they are now receiving a second publication, in only slightly altered form, more than a third of a century after they were first written.

Some word of explanation and apology is due from an author who becomes an accomplice in any such act of literary disinterment. In casting about for the most appropriate way of discharging that obligation, I began by asking myself: How did I ever come to write about the legal fiction anyway? What drew me to this theme?

Several things, I think. One was its air of innocent merriment, reminiscent of Gilbert and Sullivan—a merriment rendered the more alluring by its association with one of the most solemn of human contexts, where men robed in black sit in judgment on their fellows. The whole subject is, indeed, infused with a certain puckishness. One of the most quoted passages from Dickens, be it remembered, relates to a legal fiction. If the fiction itself has literary appeal, it seems also to stir eloquence in those who have occasion to comment on it. Even so sober-sided a writer as Austin was moved to ascribe certain legal fictions to "the active and sportive fancies of their grave and venerable authors." Bentham's unequaled capacity for excoriation was brought to full flower by the subject: "Fiction of use to justice? Exactly as swindling is to trade." In his *Rationale of Judicial Evidence* Bentham argued with at least pretended seriousness that members of the English judiciary, like convicted perjurers, should be barred from testifying on grounds of "habitual mendacity." One familiar with the intensity of the reactions engendered by the legal fiction could hardly escape some temptation to sound out his own adrenal responses to the subject. Finally, at the time when I began to study the literature of fictions, the subject was surrounded by the romantic aura of Hans Vaihinger's *Philosophy of As If,* with its mysterious title promising obscurely some mind-expanding reorientation of human perspectives.

I cannot say that these attractions were without some effect on me. I like to think, however, that my concern for the fiction arose from a more serious and more consciously oriented kind of interest. I can best express the nature of this interest by suggesting that the fiction represents the pathology of the law. When all goes well and established legal rules encompass neatly the social life they are intended to regulate, there is little occasion for fictions. There is also little occasion for philosophizing, for the law then proceeds with a transparent simplicity suggesting no need for reflective scrutiny. Only in illness, we are told, does the body reveal its complexity. Only when legal reasoning falters and reaches out clumsily for help do we realize what a complex undertaking the law is.

Changing the figure, we may liken the fiction to an awkward patch applied to a rent in the law's fabric of theory. Lifting the patch we may trace out the patterns of tension that tore the fabric and at the same time discern elements in the fabric itself that were previously obscured from view. In all this we may gain a new insight into the problems involved in subjecting the recalcitrant realities of human life to the constraints of a legal order striving toward unity and systematic structure.

In a talk given before the American Philosophical Association in 1912, Morris Cohen urged his professional colleagues to give more attention to the philosophy of law. In discussing the relevance of jurisprudence for epistemology and metaphysics he said:[1]

> Consider how much would our controversy over the nature of truth have been enriched if, instead of our easy dichotomous division of propositions into the true and false, we had taken notice of what lawyers call legal fictions. Such propositions occur, for instance, when we say that the constitution is the will of the people, or that the judges simply declare and never make the law, or when we say that the innocent purchaser of a chattel subject to mortgage has had notice of this fact if only the mortgage is duly recorded. These propositions, like the statement of the actor, "I am thy father's spirit," are not adequately characterized when we say merely that they are true or that they are false.

The fiction, in other words, forces upon our attention the relation between theory and fact, between concept and reality, and reminds us of the complexity of that relation. Curiously enough, the fiction finds its most pervasive application in two subjects that seem in other respects at opposite poles from one another: physics and jurisprudence. To be sure, fictions are to be found in other subjects, such as political science and economics, where we encounter the fictions of the social compact and the economic man. But these may be called Big Fictions. They furnish a kind of general starting point, an original impetus, to thought; they are not like the numerous little fictions of law and physics, which proliferate into the interstices of their subject and enter intimately into its every-

[1] "Jurisprudence as a Philosophical Discipline," 1913, *10 J. Phil., Psych. and Sci. Method,* 225, 227.

day concerns. Thus the physicist may say, "For this purpose we regard light as corpuscular; for this other purpose we must regard it as wavelike." The judge, in turn, may find himself forced to declare, "For purpose x we must deem the marriage between A and B to be valid; for purpose y it is to be deemed null and void." There is nothing like this—certainly not in the same measure—in chemistry, botany, sociology, political science, or economics.

What is the reason for this difference? What characteristic sets law and physics apart from other branches of human study? I suggest it is their commitment to *comprehensive system*. When in actual life men are observed behaving in ways that seem to contradict the motives of the economic man, economists can say, "This simply illustrates the limitations of our science. We do not assert that men are motivated exclusively by the desire for economic advantage; we simply say that economics is concerned with their actions only insofar as they are so motivated." No such easy way out is available to law and physics. The physicist cannot—at least openly and comfortably—say, "Of course this newly observed phenomenon does not fit our theories, but this simply means that it falls outside the area of our concern." The judge cannot say, "For the litigation now before me there happen to be no clearly formulated legal rules, so I shall simply leave it undecided."

To be sure, the physicist can, as it were, put the observed irregularity on the shelf and reserve it for later treatment. The judge can say, "The facts of the case before me fall outside the constraints of established law; I shall therefore decide for the defendant and dismiss the plaintiff's complaint." But at best these easy dispositions can only be temporary. In physics new discoveries are likely to break down any neat division between established theory and the inconvenient facts of nature; sooner or later, the scientist knows, he will have to face a reexamination of his whole body of theory. In law the pressure of new cases, presenting varied situations of fact, will in time compel the judge either to clarify rules previously obscure or to draw with some precision the line at which the constraints of law leave off. Neither task is easy.

A frequent and pervasive resort to fiction marks, then, those subjects where the urge toward systematic structure is strong and insistent. In recent decades, the impulse toward comprehensive system has been relaxed in all branches of human thought. Holistic views have come into disfavor, at least with analytical philosophers who view from above—or is it from without?—the various specialized fields of intellectual endeavor. The prevailing philosophy of science has tended to emphasize *prediction* rather than *comprehension,* the latter term being understood here in a double sense. By the standards of this philosophy, acquiring the ability to predict what will happen in some isolated context is more significant than developing a general theory which, though it seems to explain much, confronts unresolved anomalies. In the social sciences behavioristic and associationist conceptions not only have worked almost explicitly against general theory, but have made men indifferent to unresolved incongruities among molecular explanations. In ethics the philosophy of utilitarianism has adopted as the foundation for moral theory the unstructured and discrete regularities observable in the things that make men feel good. Legal philosophy has tended to disregard the institutional processes that bring law into being and produce its efficacy in human affairs; legal scholars have talked about the rules that emerge from those processes rather than about "the law" itself, this term having in consequence acquired an aura of outmoded naïveté. A general antipathy to metaphysics has barred any inquiry into the nature of "reality." The result has been to obscure the kind of problem the fiction is intended to solve, that of bridging a gap between concept and reality, between understanding and the thing sought to be understood.

There are signs that what has been called the Age of Analysis is coming to a close. If this prognosis is correct, the reaction will no doubt be accompanied by its own peculiar forms of excess. It seems unlikely, however, that men will remain content indefinitely to examine and reexamine the conceptual apparatus they project on reality without asking themselves more about the nature of that reality.

Among portents of a change in our intellectual climate one may cite Michael Polanyi's *The Logic of Liberty* (1951) and his *Personal Knowledge* (1958), as well as Thomas Kuhn's *The Structure of Scientific Revolutions* (1962). Also standing like a huge question mark over the whole analytical school is W. V. Quine's unrefuted and still imperfectly absorbed challenge to the distinction between analytic and synthetic judgments (*From a Logical Point of View*, 1953, pp. 20–46). When works like these have been absorbed, it is likely that the urge toward *comprehension*—again, in a double sense— will reassert itself.

I trust that the slightly cosmic flavor of these last paragraphs will not suggest that the present book offers any serious contribution to the philosophy of mind. Its claims are far more modest. For the legal scholar, it may serve as a reminder that the legal fiction is a more complex phenomenon than he is ordinarily inclined to suppose; more generally, it may remind him that judges do not simply "make" law in the simple and direct way modern commentators often seem to assume. For the reader not trained in the law, the book may offer some useful perspectives into the nature of legal thought.

In preparing the text for its present publication I have concentrated chiefly on de*very*fication, that is, pruning out needless adjectives and superlatives. I have made little attempt to bring the work up to date. Much of the physics in the third chapter is now archaic. But I think it safe to say that as the frontiers of science have advanced, fictions and other like intellectual dodges have followed closely behind. The context may be different, but the problems remain much as they were. In any event, I console myself with the thought that a reader interested enough to read a book, even a small book, about fictions must be tolerant of allegory. So I ask of the reader that he regard as allegorical anything he encounters in this book (including *The Philosophy of As If*) that seems to him to bear too plainly the marks of its age.

Legal Fictions

1. What Is a Legal Fiction?

Probably no lawyer would deny that judges and writers on legal topics frequently make statements they know to be false. These statements are called "fictions." There is scarcely a field of the law in which one does not encounter one after another of these conceits of the legal imagination. Sometimes they take the form of pretenses as obvious and guileless as the "let's play" of children.[1] At other times they assume a more subtle character and effect their entrance into the law under the cover of such grammatical disguises as "the law presumes," "it must be implied," "the plaintiff must be deemed," etc. Nor is it true, as is sometimes tacitly assumed, that fictions are to be found only in court decisions, where they are the product of the peculiar situation of the judge, who must, or feels he must, to some extent obscure the true nature of his activities. Fictions are to be found not only in the opinions of judges, but in critical treatises written by men free from any of the influences that supposedly restrain the judge and warp his expression. Even the austere science of jurisprudence has not found it possible to dispense with fic-

---

[1] Cf. Pound, *Interpretations of Legal History* (1923), p. 4. "From time to time they make the inevitable readjustments . . . by fictions often comparable to the 'let's play' this and that of children."

tion. The influence of the fiction extends to every department of the jurist's activities.

Yet it cannot be said that this circumstance has ever caused the legal profession much embarrassment. Laymen frequently complain of the law; they very seldom complain that it is founded upon fictions. They are more apt to express discontent when the law has refused to adopt what they regard as an expedient and desirable fiction. Perhaps, too, the fiction has played its part in making the law "uncognoscible" to the layman. The very strangeness and boldness of the legal fiction has tended to stifle his criticisms, and has no doubt often led him to agree modestly with the writer of Sheppard's Touchstone, that "the subject matter of law is somewhat transcendent, and too high for ordinary capacities."[2]

Within the profession itself there has been for a long time a consciousness of the importance of the legal fiction, and some attempt has been made to evaluate it critically. The prevailing opinion has been that suggested in Ihering's statement, "It is easy to say, 'Fictions are makeshifts, crutches to which science ought not to resort.' So soon as science can get along without them, certainly not! But it is better that science should go on crutches than to slip without them, or not to venture to move at all."[3] The fiction has generally been regarded as something of which the law ought to be ashamed, and yet with which the law cannot, as yet, dispense.

Bentham was almost unremitting in his attacks. He detected everywhere "the pestilential breath of Fiction."[4] "In English law, fiction is a syphilis, which runs in every vein, and carries into every part of the system the principle of

---

[2] Preface (6th ed., 1791), p. xiii.

[3] Ihering, *Geist des römischen Rechts auf den verschiedenen Stufen seiner Entwicklung* (6th ed., 1924), III[1], 297. (In this and all subsequent quotations from German and French treatises [except where the citation is to a published English translation] the translations are my own, and in some cases are rather free.)

[4] *Works* (Bowring's edition, 1843), I, 235.

rottenness."[5] "Fiction of use to justice? Exactly as swindling is to trade."[6] "The most pernicious and basest sort of lying."[7] "It affords presumptive and conclusive evidence of moral turpitude in those by whom it was invented and first employed."[8] "It has never been employed but with a bad effect."[9] These quotations will serve to show his temper. And yet even Bentham could not escape making the cautious admission that, "With respect to . . . fictions, there was once a time, perhaps, when they had their use."[10]

Blackstone might be expected to stand at the opposite pole. He does refer to fictions as being "highly beneficial and useful."[11] And yet even he is not blind to the other side of the picture. In one place in particular he is inclined to be apologetic. In speaking of the fictions and pretenses involved in the common recovery he says, "To such awkward shifts, such subtile refinements, and such strange reasoning, were our ancestors obliged to have recourse . . . while we may applaud the end, we cannot admire the means."[12] At another place the only defense he can find is the doubtful one of recrimination, when he points out that the common-law fictions were no worse than the numerous fictions of the Roman law.[13]

One finds frequently the criticism that a certain doctrine of the courts is based on a fiction. This is assumed, without demonstration, to furnish an argument against the doctrine. And yet frequently we find the same critics passing over one fiction after another without the slightest animadversion; oc-

---

[5] *Ibid.*, V, 92.
[6] *Ibid.*, VII, 283.
[7] *Ibid.*, VI, 582.
[8] *Ibid.*, IX, 77.
[9] *Ibid.*
[10] *Ibid.*, I, 268. It should be said that Bentham was here speaking of the fiction of the social compact, and not of legal fictions in the stricter sense.
[11] *Commentaries* (Lewis ed., 1897), III, *43.
[12] *Ibid.*, II, *360.
[13] *Ibid.*, III, *107.

casionally with commendatory remarks. What is even more significant, it is seldom that the authors of such criticisms are able to avoid occasional resort to fiction in the formulation of their own views. I take as an example one of our best writers; I choose him simply because he is one of our best. This writer rejects the notion that "implied conditions" in contract rest upon the intent of the parties, on the ground that "it is an obvious fiction" and adds the warning, "It is better to state the law in terms of reality, for misapprehension is sure to be caused by fiction."[14] Yet the same writer in another place in the same work, in commenting on the rule that a judgment in favor of the principal when he is sued by the creditor in certain cases bars the creditor from proceeding against the surety—a rule that involves a departure from the ordinary principles of *res adjudicata*—does not hesitate to make the suggestion, "The solution for the difficulty is this . . . the creditor must be deemed in fault for having suffered judgment to go against him, and . . . like a creditor who has released the principal, he will lose his right against the surety."[15] Truly, "the bogey of the fiction revenges itself often bitterly on those who would track it down!"[16]

What should we do about the fiction? Should we attempt to restate the law "in terms of reality?" Could we succeed in such an attempt? Are there good and bad fictions? If so, how are we to tell the one from the other? These are the questions I shall attempt to answer. I propose that this skeleton in the family of the law be taken from its closet and examined thoroughly. After that examination we may decide what we

[14] Williston on *Contracts* (1st ed., 1920), II, 1576–77.
[15] *Ibid.*, p. 2284. Professor Williston includes certain qualifications in his statement which modify, but do not destroy, its fictitious character. For example, he would make the inference of "fault" on the part of the creditor only when the principal debtor "did not have on the actual facts a defense to the action against him." But does absence of a defense on the part of the principal debtor conclusively show "fault" on the part of the creditor who loses the suit?
[16] Ihering, III[1], 310.

ought to do with it. At any event I am convinced that keeping it in the closet is both dangerous and unbecoming.

It is obvious that a critical evaluation of the fiction as a device of legal thought and expression cannot be undertaken until one has at least attempted an answer to the question: What *is* a fiction? It scarcely need be said that this question is not an easy one. To anyone who has thought about the matter, questions like the following must at some time have occurred. "This doctrine which I have criticized as a fiction, is it not simply the figurative expression of a truth? If I recast the expression of it, and emasculate it by removing the metaphorical elements from it, have I really accomplished anything of importance? I have called this other statement a fiction. Do I not simply mean that it is a plain falsehood, rendered harmless by its utter incapacity to deceive? At other times when I use the word 'fiction' do I mean anything more than 'bad reasoning'?" The possibility of questions such as these suggests that the word "fiction," like most words, may not always mean the same thing.

And yet, however difficult it may be at times to draw the line, a fiction (if the word is to retain any utility) is neither a truthful statement, nor a lie, nor an erroneous conclusion. In attempting to draw the line a little more clearly, it will be convenient to start with a discussion of the problem:[17]

A Fiction Distinguished from a Lie

Ihering once called fictions the "white lies" of the law.[18] This statement is probably more clever than accurate, unless we interpret "white lies" to mean falsehoods which are not

[17] It would perhaps be well to remind the reader that I am concerned not merely with what we may call the typical legal fiction, i.e., the procedural pretense by means of which rules of law are changed (e.g., the bill of Middlesex; the fictions involved in ejectment, trover, and the other actions). I am also dealing with the more subtle and less obvious kinds of fictions. If the discussion were confined to procedural pretenses, the distinctions about to be discussed would be so obvious as to render extended discussion of them unnecessary.

[18] Ihering, III[1], 305.

meant to be believed. For a fiction is distinguished from a lie by the fact that it is not intended to deceive.

It may be objected that as to that large class of fictions which we call historical fictions this generalization does not hold. Maine's classical definition of the historical fiction as "any assumption which conceals, or affects to conceal, the fact that a rule of law has undergone alteration, its letter remaining unchanged, its operation being modified,"[19] seems to leave room for the intent to deceive. The English courts were in the habit of pretending that a chattel, which might in fact have been taken from the plaintiff by force, had been *found* by the defendant.[20] Why? In order to allow an action which otherwise would not have lain. If this fiction does not deceive, of what purpose is it?

The answer is that the fiction, *as such*, was not intended to deceive and did not deceive anyone. No one believed that the chattel had been found by the defendant simply because the pleadings said so; the fact was known to be otherwise. The deceit, if any, consisted in the concealment by the court of the exercise of legislative power under the guise of this pretense. Or, perhaps more accurately stated—since it is hardly conceivable that those living contemporaneously with the development of this fiction could have been unaware that the law was changing—the deceit consisted in the representation that an expansion of the action of trover under this pretense was legitimate. This representation, however, was probably as heartily believed by the authors of the fiction as anyone else. It is easy to conclude uncharitably that the judge who enlarges his jurisdiction or who changes a rule of law under

[19] Maine, *Ancient Law* (1861; Beacon Press ed., 1963), p. 25. Cf. "the authorities . . . distinctly admit that fiction is frequently resorted to in the attempt to conceal the fact that the law is undergoing alteration in the hands of the judges." J. Smith, "Surviving Fictions," 27 *Yale L. Jour.* (1917), 147, 150.

[20] Blackstone, III, *152.

cover of a fiction is very coolly and calculatingly choosing to hide from the public the fact that he is legislating. What is usually overlooked is that he himself is often acting under the influence of some half-articulate philosophy of law which seems to him to justify the change if it takes place under the apparent sanction of old formulas, when it would not be justified otherwise.

Conceding, however, that this may not always be the case, and that the fiction may at times have been implicated in a process of deceit that was not simply self-deceit, the fact remains that the pretense or assumption involved in the fiction itself (e.g., that the defendant found the plaintiff's chattel) has never been made with the intention of producing belief in *its* truth. The fiction, *as such,* is not intended to deceive. It may, perhaps, be held accountable as accomplice in a process of deception, but not as principal.

A Fiction Distinguished from an Erroneous Conclusion

A fiction is generally distinguished from an erroneous conclusion (or in scientific fields, from a false hypothesis) by the fact that it is adopted by its author with knowledge of its falsity. A fiction is an "expedient, but *consciously false,* assumption."[21]

Taking this as a criterion, if a statement is believed by its author it is not a fiction. But what is "believing"? How many of us, in discussing a legal problem, have had the experience of making a statement with a vague feeling in the back of our minds that our expression was in some unexplained way inadequate, inaccurate—even fictitious—without being able at the time to formulate the precise nature of this inadequacy? On such occasions, lacking the time or the mental energy for a more complete analysis, we are apt to rush on in the devout

[21] Vaihinger, *Die Philosophie des Als Ob* (4th ed., 1920), p. 130.

hope that the half-consciously-felt defect in our expression
could be shown not to affect the validity of the statement in
its context. We trust that our statement is at least metaphorically true. When we do this, however, we must be prepared
to have someone else attach the epithet "fiction" to our statement.

The line between belief and disbelief is frequently blurred.
The use of the word "fiction" does not always imply that the
author of the statement positively disbelieved it. It may rather
imply the opinion that the author of the statement in question
was (or would have been had he seen its full implication)
aware of its inadequacy or partial untruth, although he may
have believed it in the sense that he could think of no better
way of expressing the idea he had in mind. We have a fiction,
then, when the author of the statement either positively dis-
believes it or is partially conscious of its untruth or inadequacy.

But even with this qualification it may be questioned
whether current usage confines the concept "fiction" within
the limits suggested. Reference has already been made to
the question of "implied conditions" in contract. The earlier
view was that these conditions were dependent upon the
actual intent of the parties, and that courts in laying down
these conditions were really interpreting and construing the
contract.[22] This view has been criticized as a fiction.[23] What
we are at present interested in is, why is the word "fiction"
used here? Does it imply the opinion that the statement was
not believed by those who made it? This is questionable.
Sergeant Williams, who gave the "intent theory" currency,

---

[22] Williams, *Notes to Saunders' Reports* (1871), I, comments on
Pordage v. *Cole,* pp. 548–56; Harriman on *Contracts* (2d ed., 1901),
sec. 315.

[23] Costigan, *Performance of Contracts* (1911), p. 8; Williston, II,
sec. 825.

may have been at least partially aware that he was dealing with an imputed or fictitious intent; but those who apply the term "fiction" to his theory do not give any indication that they are led to a choice of that word because of any conjecture concerning the subjective mental processes of the learned Sergeant. They call his theory a fiction because it is false; what he thought of it is not regarded as material.

Then why is the word "fiction" used here? Why not "erroneous reasoning," or "false assumption"? The most probable explanation is that the choice of the word "fiction" here implies a recognition that the statement under discussion, although erroneous, had a certain utility. A court by proceeding *as if it were* determining the intent of the parties will normally reach a result that is in accord with the "good sense of the case." The word "fiction," then, may sometimes mean simply a false statement having a certain utility, whether it was believed by its author or not. A fiction may be an *expedient* but false assumption.

To sum up the results of our discussion, and to attempt a definition of the fiction that will at least approximate current usage, we may say: A fiction is either (1) a statement propounded with a complete or partial consciousness of its falsity, or (2) a false statement recognized as having utility.

This definition seems on the face of things to embrace two entirely discordant elements. In the first alternative the criterion is "consciousness of falsity," in the second "utility." Yet current usage probably permits of this alternative definition. What is the explanation for this apparently unreasonable linguistic development? There is often underlying the seemingly illogical usages of language a penetrating comprehension which does not find expression in any other way. That is the case here. In practice, it is precisely those false statements that are realized as being false that have utility. A fiction taken seriously, i.e., "believed," becomes dangerous and loses its utility. It ceases to be a fiction under either alternative of the definition given above.

The "half-conscious" insight into the falsity of an assumption, which is discussed above, will normally be a sufficient guard against a harmful application of it. The now-discarded theory that conceived of conditions in contract as dependent upon the intent of the parties was workable probably because there existed this partial awareness of the untruth of its fundamental postulate. But the danger of the fiction varies inversely with the acuteness of this awareness. A fiction becomes wholly safe only when it is used with a complete consciousness of its falsity.[24]

A Fiction Distinguished from the Truth

Everyone who has dealt with legal problems must, at one time or another, have had the experience of feeling that a certain doctrine of the law was expressed in terms of fiction, and yet have found himself, to his dismay, unable to restate the doctrine without resort to fiction. At such moments one is apt to succumb to the feeling that "a fiction that we needs must feign is somehow or another very like the simple truth."[25]

A fiction is frequently a metaphorical way of expressing a truth. The truth of any given statement is only a question of its adequacy. No statement is an entirely adequate expression of reality, but we reserve the label "false" for those statements involving an inadequacy that is outstanding or unusual. The truth of a statement is, then, a question of degree.

[24] Cf. "Seeking the intention of the parties as the sole governing principle led Sergeant Williams to declare a promise independent if one performance or part of it might by the terms of the contract under some circumstances precede performance of the counter promise; and a few unjust decisions have been made in consequence." Williston, II, sec. 826.

[25] Maitland, Collected Papers (1911), III, 316. Cf. Saleilles, De la personnalité juridique (2d ed., 1922), p. 613: "Indeed, what is a fiction which becomes indispensable if not a reality?"

But we do not solve a problem by saying that it is a question of degree; what we want to know is, what factors affect this "degree" upon which the question depends? More particularly, stating the thing in a form applicable to our present problem, we are interested in an analysis of the different reasons why, in a given case, doubt may arise whether a statement is fictitious or true.

The Fiction as a Linguistic Phenomenon

Ihering once said that the History of the Law could write as a motto over her first chapter the sentence, "In the beginning was the Word."[26] Students of the legal fiction might also take this motto to heart. For certainly it is a truth commonly overlooked that the fiction is "a disease or affection of language."

Anyone who has thought about the legal fiction must be aware that it presents an illustration of the all-pervading power of the word. That a statement which is disbelieved by both its author and his audience can have any significance at all is evidence enough that we are here in contact with the mysterious influence exercised by names and symbols. In that sense the fiction is a linguistic phenomenon.

But we are interested in another aspect of the thing. The fiction is further a phenomenon of language in the sense that the question whether a given statement *is* a fiction is always, when examined critically, a question of the proprieties of language. A statement must be false before it can be a fiction. Its falsity depends upon whether the words used are inaccurate as an expression of reality. But the inaccuracy of a statement must be judged with reference to the standards of

[26] Ihering expresses in this fashion the exaggerated respect shown by early law for the written and spoken word. "Among all primitive peoples the word appears as something mysterious; a naïve faith ascribes to the word a supernatural power" (II^2, 441).

language usage. Simple as this truth is, nothing has so obscured the subject of legal fictions as the failure to recognize it.

In the law we speak of the *merger* of estates, of the *breaking* of contracts, of the *ripening* of obligations. Vivid and inappropriate are the literal connotations of these expressions—yet they are usually not even felt as metaphors. These words, and many others like them, have become naturalized in the language of the law. They have acquired a special legal significance which comes to the mind of the lawyer when they are used, so instinctively, indeed, that he is usually unaware that they have a more vivid sensual connotation.

In the action of trover the defendant is alleged to have *found* a chattel he may really have taken by force.[27] In actions arising under the "attractive nuisance doctrine" the defendant is alleged to have *invited* children (of whose very existence he may have been ignorant) to visit his premises.[28] These statements are felt as fictions. Is this because there is any inherent reason why the words used could not acquire a special sense which would make them true? Could not "finding" mean, in a technical legal sense, "taking"?[29] Could not "inviting" be extended to include "attracting"?[30] Neither of these things is impossible. But the fact simply is that these possible changes in meaning have not occurred. Since they have not, the statements remain fictions.

Most of what has been written about the supposedly profound question of corporate personality has ignored the possibility that the question discussed might be one of termi-

[27] Blackstone, III, *152.

[28] J. Smith, "Liability of Landowners to Children Entering without Permission," 11 *Harv. L. Rev.* (1898), 349, 434.

[29] Of course the word "finding" has not escaped metaphorical extension. For example, we speak of a jury "finding" the facts of the case.

[30] I do not mean to imply in this discussion that the proper basis of liability in the "attractive nuisance cases" is to be found in the notion of "attracting." My attention is directed solely toward the linguistic question.

nology merely. No one can deny that the group of persons forming a corporation is treated, legally and extralegally, as a "unit." "Unity" is always a matter of subjective convenience.[31] I may treat all the hams hanging in a butcher shop as a "unit" —their "unity" consists in the fact that they are hanging in the same butcher shop. Certainly there is a more easily explained "unity" in a corporation than there is in such everyday concepts as "the 9:10 train for Chicago." It is also clear that the corporation, taken as a unit, must be treated by the courts and legislatures in that somewhat complex fashion which we epitomize by saying that legal rights and duties are attributed to the corporation.[32] It is further clear that this treatment of the corporation bears a striking (though not complete) resemblance to that accorded "natural persons." It then follows that natural persons and corporations are to some extent treated in the same way in the law; they form a "class." There are only two questions left for discussion. The first is, is it worth while having a name for this class? It should be remembered that many classes remain nameless. The class of left-handed Irishmen still suffers from the lack of an appropriate term to separate it from the world of the right-handed, the ambidextrous, the non-Irish.[33] Assuming, however, that it is

[31] Mallachow, *Rechtserkenntnistheorie und Fiktionslehre—Das Als Ob Im Jus* (1922), p. 67.

[32] Bülow, in an article on the procedural fictions of German law ("Civilprozessualische Fiktionen und Wahrheiten," 62 *Archiv f.d. civilistische Praxis* [1879], 1, 10), says that a proper understanding of fictions ought to bring us to realize "that the incorporeal center of legal interests which we designate as a 'legal person' possesses a substantiality and independence which cannot, and need not, be created for it by an act of imagination." This "substantiality," however, need not include any such supernatural elements as a "common will."

[33] "We do not often have occasion to speak, as of an indivisible whole, of the group of phenomena involved or connected in the transit of a negro over a rail-fence with a melon under his arm while the moon is just passing behind a cloud. But if this collocation of phenomena were of frequent occurrence, and if we did have occasion to speak of it often, and if its happening were likely to affect the money market, we

worth while having a name for this common class formed by
natural persons and corporations, the other question is, is the
word "person" the most desirable name? Would "legal subject" be better? Or "right-and-duty-bearing-unit"?[34]

Live and Dead Fictions

There are live and dead fictions. A fiction dies when a compensatory change takes place in the meaning of the words
or phrases involved, which operates to bridge the gap that
previously existed between the fiction and reality.

This is a process that is going on all the time. A striking
example is to be found in Roman constitutional law. The
comitia (assembly of citizens) had, originally, only a power
of *authorizing* constitutional changes proposed to them by
the king. Their legislative function was originally essentially
negative—a power of veto. Gradually, however, they gained
the power of initiating and commanding. With this constitutional development came an interesting change in language:

> The evolution that led from the right of approval in the
> comitia to their right to command is reflected in the parallel
> evolution in the sense of the word *jubere* (in the formula
> *velitis jubeatis quirites*), which has equally passed from the
> sense of accepting to that of ordaining.[35]

The statement that the *comitia* merely accepted proposals
was originally true; it became a fiction through a change in
practice. But this fiction was in turn cured—or to change the

---

should have some name as 'wousin' to denote it by. People would in
time be disputing whether the existence of a wousin involved necessarily a rail-fence and whether the term could be applied when a white
man was similarly related to a stone wall." A. Ingraham, "Swain School
Lectures" (1903), p. 121, quoted from Ogden and Richards, *The
Meaning of Meaning* (2d ed., 1927), p. 46.

[34] The article on "Legal Personality" by Bryant Smith in 37 *Yale L.
Jour.* (1928), 283, offers a penetrating analysis of the problem.

[35] Girard, *Manuel élémentaire de droit romain* (8th ed., 1929), p.
17, n. 1.

figure, became dead—through a change in language usage.[36]

The same thing is happening in our own law. Words like "delivery" (= giving over), "conversion" and "estate" (= condition or status) have gone through like developments. There was a time, probably, when these words were applied legally in their literal sense. Then a period of extension set in, during which the continued use of these words was probably felt as fictional. But the inevitable compensatory change in word meaning took place; the expressions acquired a new, nonfictional meaning. This development is, however, not yet ended. Even today the first of these terms still carries a part of its history with it; it is not a completely dead fiction. Courts are still inclined to speak of "symbolic" or "constructive" delivery when the act in question is too far removed in character from the kind of thing contemplated by the original sense of the word. But that the fiction is dying is shown by the fact that there is no definite standard for determining when these qualifying terms are needed; it is a matter of individual discretion.

Of course this process is not confined to the law—it takes place in the whole of our language. "All words expressive of immaterial conceptions are derived by metaphor from words expressive of sensible ideas."[37] "The birth of a new concept is inevitably foreshadowed by a more or less strained or extended use of old linguistic material."[38] All the language of

---

[36] The clearest recognition of this process that I have been able to find in the literature of jurisprudence is in the following passage. "It is true that so soon as, with the passage of time, normal conceptions have changed, that which was a fiction at the beginning will have become a reality, since there will be, from that time on, a normal adaptation between the effects produced and the legal system . . . to which those effects are attributed. After all, what is a fiction which becomes indispensable if not a reality?" Saleilles, p. 613. See also Tourtoulon, *Philosophy in the Development of Law* (1922), p. 388: "very old fictions are no longer considered as such."

[37] Müller, *The Science of Language*, Second Series (1864), p. 355.

[38] Sapir, *Language* (1921), p. 16. Cf. Mallachow, p. 41: "Concepts (both the ordinary and the scientific sort) are accepted by the linguis-

abstract thought is metaphorical, but, fortunately, the metaphors involved are for the most part dead metaphors. I quote
at length from a popular book on language usage:[39]

> In all discussion of metaphors it must be borne in mind that
> some metaphors are living, i.e., are offered and accepted
> with a consciousness of their nature as substitutes for their
> literal equivalents, while others are dead, i.e., have been
> so often used that speaker and hearer have ceased to be
> aware that the words used are not literal; but the line of
> distinction between the live and the dead is a shifting one,
> the dead being sometimes liable, under the stimulus of an
> affinity or a repulsion, to galvanic stirrings indistinguish-
> able from life. Thus, in *The men were sifting meal* we have
> a literal use of *sift;* in *Satan hath desired to have you, that
> he may sift you as wheat, sift* is a live metaphor; in *the
> sifting of evidence,* the metaphor is so familiar that it is
> about equal chances whether *sifting* or *examination* will be
> used, and that a sieve is not present to the thought—unless

---

tic sense of the ordinary man as well as by science (with the exception
of epistemology) rather blindly and without preliminary examination
as something given. The question of their reality is raised only when
one may live contemporaneously with, and is conscious of, the creation
of a concept, as for example, in the formation of the general designa-
tion 'energy' or of the . . . concept of the legal person."

It should be added that this question of the "reality" of a concept is
also likely to arise in one's mind when one encounters a concept that
has been discarded in the course of history and that is therefore unfamiliar. "Seisin" seems a very unreal thing to us; we have no hesitation
in concluding that it was something that existed only in the heads of
medieval lawyers. Yet "title" and "possession" are apt to seem very real
to us; we say, "Possession passed from A to B," or, "X cannot have title
because Y has it," just as the lawyer of the year 1400 talked of seisin
passing, or, perhaps more often, refusing to pass. But in a system of law
in which important legal consequences are "attributed to" seisin—or,
stated in another way, where the word "seisin" is a way of lumping together the effects of certain legal doctrines—seisin is as real a thing as
"title" or "possession." Cf. Maitland, *Lectures on Equity* (1909), p.
33: "The use came to be conceived as *a sort of metaphysical entity.*"
(Italics mine.) A use was a "metaphysical entity" in exactly the same
sense that "legal title" is a "metaphysical entity" today.

[39] Fowler, *Modern English Usage* (1926), p. 348.

indeed someone conjures it up by saying *All the evidence must first be sifted with acid tests,* or *with the microscope*—; under such a stimulus our metaphor turns out to have been not dead but dormant; the other word, *examine,* will do well enough as an example of the real stone-dead metaphor; the Latin *examino,* being from *examen* the tongue of a balance, meant originally to weigh; but, though weighing is not done with acid tests or microscopes any more than sifting, *examine* gives no convulsive twitches, like *sift,* at finding itself in their company; *examine,* then, is dead metaphor, and *sift* only half dead, or three-quarters.

Eliminating the "fiction" from law often means only substituting dead metaphors for live ones. One sees an example of this in the following quotation: " 'Consensual' contracts, or some better term, should be used to designate those contracts where there is a real 'meeting,' i.e., coincidence, of the minds of the parties."[40] "Meeting" was felt as a metaphor, and required quotation marks accordingly. "Coincidence" (= falling on) was a dead metaphor and could stand unadorned.[41]

Nor is this sort of change in language meaning confined to single words—whole phrases may be involved. Just as the expression "sowing his wild oats" is more apt to call to mind a cabaret than a field, so it seems probable that the expression "Fact A is conclusively presumed" carries to the well-trained

[40] Costigan, "Constructive Contracts," 19 *Green Bag* (1907), 512, 514.

[41] The special utility of Latin terms consists in the fact that they are generally fictions that have never lived—in our language—at all; they are, as it were, stillborn into the language of the law. That is why we seldom see Latin expressions qualified by such apologetic adjectives as "constructive" and "implied." We speak frequently of "constructive" and "implied" *intent* because we have a feeling for the boundaries of this thoroughly naturalized word. On the other hand, although it would be just as logical to do so, we do not speak of "constructive" or "implied" *mens rea.*

legal mind the simple connotation "Fact A is legally immaterial."

The assumptions involved in the typical fiction of the
English common law, i.e., the procedural pretense, were
usually so violent that there was little likelihood that the
adoption of the fiction would usher in a change in language
usage which would cure the fiction. When the English court
pretended that the Island of Minorca was a part of the city
of London, as it once did,[42] there was little probability that
this isolated pretense would lead to a change in the meaning
of the word "London" that would extend it to embrace a spot
of land in the Mediterranean. But even procedural pretenses
may lead to the development of word meanings. The "possession" that gave the right to bring the action of trespass to
a plaintiff who had bailed his chattel under a bailment
terminable at his will was originally simply a pretense
through which a man out of possession was given a posses-
sory action. But this pretense, and others like it, became so
common that the word "possession" began to take on new
meaning and we end up with two kinds of possession, "constructive" and "actual." When we had this condition of
affairs, the inveterate tendency of the human mind to suppose that where two things have a common name they must
have something in common besides the name began to assert
itself. Legal theorists felt the need of what the Continental
jurists call a "construction." That is, it was felt that we ought
to develop some "concept" that would include, and reconcile,
all the conflicting elements to be found in actual and constructive possession. Needless to say, the concept has not yet
been discovered; the "construction" remains a matter of
difficulty.

"Constructive fraud" has had a somewhat similar history.

[42] Gray, *Nature and Sources of the Law* (1st ed., 1909), p. 34.

It started, innocently enough, as a pretense by means of which English courts of equity acquired jurisdiction over cases that would otherwise have been outside their province.[43] But the term lived beyond the causes that gave rise to it, and survives today into a period when the distinction between legal and equitable jurisdiction is generally done away with. What "constructive fraud" is today, no one knows exactly; but it is still with us.

Those who contend that "corporate personality" is and must be a fiction should be reminded that the word "person" originally meant "mask"; that its application to human beings was at first metaphorical. They would not contend that it is a fiction to say that Bill Smith is a person; their contention that "corporate personality" must necessarily involve a fiction must be based ultimately on the notion that the word "person" has reached the legitimate end of its evolution and that it ought to be pinned down where it now is.

One may test the question whether a fiction is dead or alive by the inquiry, does the statement involve a pretense? Probably the maxim "Qui facit per alium facit per se" was originally a fiction because it was understood as an invitation to the reader to pretend that the act in question had actually been done by the principal in person. But the statement has been so often repeated that it now conveys its meaning (that the principal is legally bound by the acts of the agent) *directly;* the pretense that formerly intervened between the statement and this meaning has been dropped out as a superfluous and wasteful intellectual operation. The death of a fiction may indeed be characterized as a result of the operation of the law of economy of effort in the field of mental processes.

[43] J. Smith, "Surviving Fictions," *27 Yale L. Jour.* (1918), 317, 319.

Rejection v. Redefinition

It is apparent from what has been said that there are two distinct methods of eliminating fiction from the law: *rejection* and *redefinition*. By rejection is meant simply the discarding of those statements that are felt as fictional. Thus, a statute or judicial decision may declare that henceforth the action of ejectment shall be allowed without the allegations of lease, entry, and ouster. By redefinition is meant a change in word meaning that eliminates the element of pretense; to preserve the figure used before, redefinition results in the death of the fiction. Through rejection a fiction disappears entirely; through redefinition it becomes a part of the technical vocabulary of the law.

Both of these processes have taken place in the past. Although the legal language of today is in part, at least, composed of the dead shells of former pretenses ("possession," "conversion," "delivery," "estate," "person," "constructive fraud," "constructive trust"), there are many fictions of former days which have disappeared completely, which have left no vestigial traces in the language of the law. This fact suggests the inquiry: why, in the course of history, are some fictions discarded entirely, while others are redefined and retained as terms of description? And the fact that the alternative fates of rejection and redefinition rest in the balance for many of our present-day fictions suggests the question, which of these processes—rejection or redefinition—ought we to encourage?

Would it, for example, be desirable to attempt a complete elimination of fiction from the law by a wholesale process of redefinition? Conceivably we might eliminate the pretense from all of our fictions; we might cease to say, "A is legally treated as if it were B," and simply say, "In a technical legal sense, A *is* B." We might say, "There is no pretense in actions arising under the 'attractive nuisance doctrine'; the word 'inviting,' as used in those decisions, is to be understood in a technical legal sense." We could do this with the boldest of our fictions. The English court that declared the Island of Minorca to be a part of London might have defended itself by saying, "We only meant that for the special purpose at hand the island was a part of London, and we defy anyone to prove that that is not so." In short, we might join Humpty Dumpty in saying, "When I use a word, it means just what I choose it to mean, neither more nor less." We might erect a legal world in which silence *is* consent, taking *is* finding, attracting *is* inviting, to bring a suit *is* to achieve Roman citizenship; a world in which even the commonest expressions were to be understood in a Pickwickian sense. This attitude has, indeed, been dignified by a name—"the theory of the juristic truth of fictions."[44]

But it is clear enough that such a wholesale process of redefinition could not be carried out. One cannot introduce sweeping changes in linguistic usage by an arbitrary fiat; in general, new meanings grow only in places where they are needed. And even if it were possible, the proposal ought not to be carried out because it would only result in encumbering the language of the law with a grotesque assemblage of technical concepts lacking the slightest utility.

Is the alternative, then, a wholesale rejection of fictions? This is also impossible, and inadvisable if it were possible. It is *inadvisable* because to reject all of our fictions would be to put legal terminology in a straitjacket—fictions are, to a

[44] The "theory of juristic truth" is discussed by Franz Bernhöft in his book *Zur Lehre von den Fiktionen* (1907) and by Bülow in an article in 62 *Archiv f.d. civilistische Praxis*, 1. Cf. Saleilles, p. 612: "We see then clearly that, from the moment when one introduces into the sphere of law an element of intellectual conceptualism, a portion of conventionalism, one is tempted to say that there are no fictions at all, and that, in every legal relation, from the moment it is accepted as such, there is a reality of law."

certain extent, simply the growing pains of the language of
the law. It is *impossible* because fiction, in the sense of a
"strained use of old linguistic material," is an inevitable
accompaniment of progress in the law itself and this progress
can scarcely be expected to wait out of deference for the
tastes of those who experience an unpleasant sensation at the
sight of words browsing beyond their traditional pastures.

The solution lies between the extremes. Some fictions
should be rejected; some should be redefined. Redefinition
is proper where it results in the creation of a useful concept—
where the dead (redefined) fiction fills a real linguistic need.
Where this is not so, rejection may be the proper course to
pursue. But what are "useful concepts"? How does it come
about that redefinition in some cases results in a needed
addition to the terminology of the law; in other cases serves
only to preserve a bizarre reminder of a discarded pretense?
A discussion of these problems must be postponed until later
when an attempt will be made to analyze the fiction from the
standpoint of *motives*. When we have discovered *why* courts
and legal writers resort to fiction we shall be in a better position to deal with the problem of the utility of particular
fictions.

For our present purposes it is enough to notice that the
evolution of our legal language has, for the most part, proceeded along the lines suggested. In general, only those
fictions that, when redefined, yield useful concepts have
been retained. The linguistic sense of generations of lawyers
has been, in the main, adequate to sift the chaff from the
wheat and to keep the language of the law safe from the opposing disasters of linguistic stagnation and a grotesque
fecundity.

The development has—in general—been sound. But there
are important exceptions—exceptions that ought sufficiently
to demonstrate the possibility that the linguistic sense of a
profession can run amok. "Constructive fraud," "constructive

trust," "constructive possession,"[45] "constructive intent," "implied malice"—these expressions stand out like ugly scars in the language of the law, the linguistic wounds of discarded make-believes. Is it not significant that each carries still the badge of its shame—the apologetic "constructive" or "implied"?

Conservative Tendencies Regarding the Growth of Technical Legal Meanings

It has just been said that the need of the law for an adequate technical vocabulary makes it desirable that certain of our fictions—picked with discretion—be converted into "juristic truth." Speaking in general terms, it is desirable to speed the growth of technical legal meanings. But it would not be well to be optimistic of sudden success in this direction. For every legal word that has been able to disencumber itself of its burden of extralegal connotation, there are ten words that carry with them into the law a mass of nonjuristic associations—frequently with the result that their legal use continues to be felt as fictitious. There are forces of conservatism that operate to hamper and restrict the natural process of language development, which I have sketched above.

One thing that works against the development of technical legal meanings is, of course, simply ignorance. It is precisely those who are misled and injured by the extralegal connotations of law words who are unconscious of the danger involved.[46] They cannot be expected to see the need for redefinition and reform.

---

[45] I am speaking here of constructive possession in the remedial sense. I do not include in this condemnation the "constructive possession" that is attributed to one who enters upon a part of a tract of land under color of title to the whole.

[46] Tourtoulon (p. 391) says rather bluntly but with some truth, "If a jurist were found for whom it was difficult to grasp the exact import

But much more important than this, in my opinion, is the tendency that I may call the desire to keep the form of the law persuasive. Metaphor is the traditional device of persuasion. Eliminate metaphor from the law and you have reduced its power to convince and convert.

"Constructive notice" will do as an illustration here. This expression has been striving for a long time to achieve a purely technical meaning, through which it would be completely divorced from the notion of a pretense of actual notice. So understood, the expression would offer a convenient way of grouping together a somewhat complex set of cases, in which a person who has no actual notice of an interest or event receives the same treatment at the hands of the law as the person who has actual notice. But such a conception, being a matter of analysis and classification entirely, offers—in contrast to "actual notice"—no "reason" for the result at all. It is much easier to see why a man should be affected adversely by "actual notice" than it is to discover the reasons that underlie the treatment he receives in cases of "constructive notice." Frequently the considerations that are determinative here are rather remote "reasons of policy." How remote they may be in a given case is shown by the fact that in some jurisdictions one may, through the operation of the recording statute, be charged with constructive notice of a deed which in fact never got on the record.[47] "Actual notice" is, then, a persuasive term; "constructive notice" is not. But we can make "constructive notice" more appealing if we preserve the notion that it has something in common with "actual notice" besides a name. If we can create the impression of a similarity (in fact and not simply in legal effect) between "actual" and "constructive" notice, we will have

---

of fictions, one who was incapable of understanding what the artifice may legitimately give and what it may not, he would do well to renounce law, as well as every other abstract science."

[47] Tiffany on *Real Property* (2d ed., 1920), II, sec. 567j.

established for the latter term a kind of vicarious persuasive force.

One way to do this is to state "constructive notice" in the form of "actual notice" proved inferentially, and to speak of "implied notice."[48] But the trouble with this expression is that it has been used in this way for so long that it begins to lose its persuasive power. The word "implied" is itself becoming a dead fiction. It is now generally understood (except when qualified by the words "in fact") as being substantially the equivalent of "constructive," i.e., as having the function of indicating that the word it modifies is to be understood in a technical legal sense. It no longer serves to create in the hearer's mind the suggestion of an actual fact proved inferentially; the insinuation contained in the word fails to take effect.

The only method left of preserving for constructive notice the superior persuasive quality of actual notice is the rather naïve device of a pretense of actual notice. The obviousness of this expedient makes it rather uncommon, but occasionally we find courts saying things like the following: "The deed was on record, and the defendant . . . must be presumed to have searched the record and come to a knowledge of the contents of the deed."[49]

Sometimes more ingenuity is employed in obfuscating the distinction between actual and constructive notice, as the following quotation will show: "Constructive notice I take

[48] One American judge went a step further and spoke of "implied actual notice," which he defines as "that which one . . . is in duty bound to seek to know" (*Hopkins* v. *McCarthy* [1921] 121 Me. 27, 29; 115 Atl. 513, 515). May we expect "constructive actual notice" next?

[49] *Digman* v. *McCollom* (1871) 47 Mo. 372, 374. We have an expression of a similar tendency in those cases where the constructive notice of the principal (through actual notice to the agent) is based upon a presumption that the agent has in fact communicated the fact in question to his principal. See Mechem on *Agency* (2d ed., 1914), II, sec. 1806(b).

to be in its nature no more than evidence of notice, the presumptions of which are so violent that the court will not allow even of its being controverted."[50]

What can be the motive of this obscurantism, which talks of "evidence" that cannot be controverted? Is it not plainly an inordinate desire to preserve the appearance of a likeness between "actual" and "constructive" notice, even at the cost of good sense? Instances like this show how far the human mind is willing to go to preserve a comforting and persuasive analogy.

The whole field of vicarious liability is a branch of the law which, from its infancy, has been honeycombed with fictions, and—what is more significant—with fictions that seem to resist the linguistic process of redefinition, with fictions that stubbornly refuse to die. Does not the explanation for this lie in the fact that the notion of vicarious liability is itself a bitter pill to swallow? The social foundations of vicarious liability are never of the self-apparent type. The harshness involved in visiting the consequences of one man's misdeeds upon another has seemed to call for repeated explanation and apology.

One further point deserves special emphasis. I have spoken of "the desire to keep the form of the law persuasive." This should not be understood as implying the existence of a studied and premeditated attitude directed toward third persons. The judge who resorts to an artifical form of statement which insinuates the existence of actual notice in a case where it is clear no actual notice exists has not consciously weighed the advantages of clarity against those of rhetoric. If he chooses metaphor to dry legal fact, it is because the former mode of expression suits his personal taste and has been successful in winning over his own conscience.

[50] Eyre, Chief Baron, in *Plumb* v. *Fluitt* (1791) 2 Anst. 432, 438.

It should be recalled, too, that rhetoric is frequently an intellectual shortcut. It is often a matter of the greatest difficulty to frame a satisfactory exposition of reasons that one feels—inarticulately—are sound. At such times metaphor offers a tempting expedient. The desire to keep the form of the law persuasive is frequently the impulse to preserve a form of statement that will make the law acceptable to those who do not have the time or the capacity for understanding reasons that are not obvious—and this class sometimes includes the author of the statement himself.

Fictitious Legal Relations

So far our discussion has concerned pretenses about facts and events that are regarded as giving rise to legal consequences. But assuming the facts to be nonfictitious, may we not also have pretenses concerning the legal consequences to be attributed to those facts? May there not be feigned legal relations, fictitious legal rights and duties, supposititious titles? The difficulty we encounter at the outset is that in dealing with words like "right," "duty," and "title" we have to do with concepts of a somewhat indefinite scope. The assertion is made that a creditor whose debt has been "barred" by the statute of limitations still has a "right."[51] Some, perhaps, would regard this assertion as inaccurate and misleading. But can it be disproved? Can the boundaries of the concept "legal right" be so rigidly drawn as to exclude a sense of the word that would make this statement true? Or again, it is said that the possessor of a trade secret has no "property right" or "title" in his process (the protection accorded him by the law being explained as an application of contract principles).[52] Many would regard the statement

---

[51] Williston, III, sec. 2002.
[52] Chafee, *Cases on Equitable Relief against Torts* (1924), p. 87, note.

(that the possessor of the secret has no "property" in it) as a mere quibbling with words. But is the assertion demonstrably untrue?

The uncertainty and flexibility inherent in legal concepts has this consequence: it is generally more difficult to say that a given statement is false when it relates purely to legal concepts than when it relates to extralegal fact. Consequently, it is not common that a statement concerning legal relations is regarded as a fiction. For example, it is a very common thing for courts to employ expressions like the following: "Title, as between the parties, had passed to the mortgagee; as to third parties, title remained in the mortgagor."[53] What kind of title is this which is both in, and not in, the grantor and the grantee at the same time? Does not such a contradictory assertion deserve the disparaging epithet "fiction"? It is doubtful if the term would ordinarily be applied to this kind of statement.[54] "Title" is itself a concept of great flexibility, serving simply as a means of grouping together certain rather complex legal results in a convenient formula. One is not apt to see any element of pretense in the statement quoted. It

[53] Statements of this kind are very common in the so-called "title" states. See *Ellison* v. *Daniels* (1840) 11 N.H. 274.

[54] Apparently many French jurists would be willing to regard a statement of this sort as a fiction. For example, sec. 1446 of their Code has frequently been regarded as establishing a fiction (Lecocq, *De la fiction comme procédé juridique* [1914], pp. 158–62). This is because the effect of this section is most succinctly stated by saying that, as to the creditors of the wife, the "community" (of the property of husband and wife) is regarded as dissolved, while as to all other persons it is considered as still subsisting.

One gets the impression that the French writers are rather ready to apply the term "fiction" to any sort of legal construction that involves the notion of substitution or comparison. Perhaps they are influenced by the example of their own Code. Section 739 provides: "Representation [i.e., in cases of succession to the goods of an intestate] *is a legal fiction* of which the effect is to have the representatives take the place, the degree, and the rights of the person whom they represent." What is the fiction?

is regarded simply as an attempt to describe, with as little circumlocution as possible, a complex legal situation.

Legal facts, then, differ from extralegal facts (at least from those extralegal facts that concern the law) in the circumstance that their boundaries are generally less certain. But this is a difference of degree only. There are limits to the elasticity of even legal concepts. For example, suppose the parties to a contract stipulate that for their purposes the title to a piece of land should be treated as if it were in A, although the courts have adjudicated it to be in B. Conceivably they may do this as a convenient way of expressing the result they seek to attain by their contract, in full awareness of the falsity of the supposition. We would not hesitate to call their statement false. We might regard it as a kind of private fiction established between the contracting parties.

But this leaves unanswered a further question: Is there any utility in speaking of fictitious legal rights and duties, or of fictitious titles, when we are speaking of statements made in court decisions? The existence of legal rights and duties depends upon how courts and their enforcement agencies act. If the judge and the sheriff act upon a "pretended" right and enforce it, is there any utility in continuing to treat it as a pretended right? If a statute declares that the courts shall treat A "as if" he had title to certain property, and the courts consistently act upon that assumption, is there any purpose in treating A's title as imaginary?[55]

A legal right reaches objectivity through court action; we have no other test of its "reality." If it meets this test, it is a real right—whatever may be the protestations of the agency enforcing it.

---

[55] The contrary view is supported by Bernhöft in his treatise, p. 19. But a careful reading of his discussion will show, I think, that he really has in mind cases where the description of the legal relation adopted by

*When Is a Statement a Statement of Fact, and When Is It
One of Legal Relations?*

Many an intellectual battle over the question whether a
given statement should be regarded as a fiction might have
been avoided if the contestants had taken the trouble to inquire whether the statement in question purported to relate
to extralegal facts, or referred to the legal relations of the
parties. Section 1890 of the German Civil Code provides, "An
illegitimate child and its father are not deemed to be related."[56] In the original draft of the code the section read
simply, "An illegitimate child and its father are unrelated."
The notion of the drafters was simply that relationship was
a legal matter; if the Code provided that they were unrelated, they *were* unrelated, and there was no need for any
apologetic "deemed." It was pointed out, however, that "relationship" is also a state of fact, and that the ordinary meaning of the word comprehends this factual state rather than
the legal relation. It was therefore thought preferable to treat
the thing in terms of a fiction of a lack of factual relationship.[57] This illustration indicates sufficiently the nature of the

---

the courts is misleading and inaccurate, the type of case discussed in
the section on "Legal Relations Described Metaphorically or Inade-
quately," *infra*, p. 33.

[56] "Ein uneheliches Kind und dessen Vater gelten nicht als Ver-
wandt."

[57] Bernhöft, p. 21. Cf. "When the common law refused to recognize
any paternity for an illegitimate son, and said he was *filius nullius,* it
was not understood to deny the fact of physiological begetting; it was
asserting that such a one did not possess the specific rights which belong
to one who was *filius,* implying wedlock as a legal institution." Dewey,
"The Historic Backgrounds of Corporate Legal Personality," 35 *Yale L.
Jour.* (1926), 655, 656.

"In a discussion of legitimacy [and the presumption that a child born
in wedlock is legitimate], Lord Campbell remarked: 'So strong is the
legal presumption of legitimacy that if a white woman have a mulatto
child, although the husband is white and the supposed paramour black,
the child is presumed legitimate, if there were any opportunities for
intercourse.' Now there might, without absurdity, be a doctrine which

problem and demonstrates that the solution is often a matter of terminology.

Suppose P tells X that he has appointed A his agent to sell his horse, with full power to fix the price. P tells A, the agent, that he must not sell the horse for less than $100. X buys the horse from A for $50. Is P bound by this act? The answer of the authorities is in the affirmative: A had an "apparent authority" to fix the price of the horse. Is this "authority" a fiction?[58] If, by saying that A had "authority," we mean to pretend, for purposes of effecting justice, that P actually stated to A that he might sell the horse for any price he thought proper, then there is a fiction. But if we mean merely that on the facts A has the legal power to sell the horse and bind P, then there is no fiction.

The same considerations are easily seen to underlie the following questions (the list might be greatly extended): When a surety pays the debt of the principal, equity considers the debt "unpaid" in order that the surety may be subrogated to the rights of the creditor.[59] Is this a fiction? Is a "constructive trust" a fiction? Is it a fiction to say, in cases arising under the "family automobile doctrine" that the son, or other member of the family, is the "agent" of the owner of the car? Section 50 of the German Civil Code provides, "The existence of the association (in liquidation) shall be deemed to continue to

---

fixed upon a husband, even under such circumstances, the legal responsibilities of a father; according to the rough proverbial wisdom, quoted by a vigorous English judge four or five centuries ago, 'who that bulleth my cow the calf is mine.' But . . . Lord Campbell had introduced into his supposition such unusual facts as dissolved and evaporated any rule of presumption." Thayer, *Preliminary Treatise on Evidence at the Common Law* (1898), pp. 346–47.

[58] In a note in *18 Harv. L. Rev.* (1905), 400, the view is taken that this authority is fictitious; Professor Cook in a rejoiner in "Agency by Estoppel: A Reply," *6 Col. L. Rev.* (1906), 34, 44, emphatically denies that any fiction is involved.

[59] Occasionally courts regard subrogation as a "resuscitation" of the security. *Thirteenth Ward Bldg. & Loan Assn.* v. *Kanter* (N.J. 1929) 147 Atl. 809, 811.

the close of the liquidation, in so far as the purpose of the liquidation requires this." Is the word "deemed" necessary here? Is it a fiction to say (in the law of divorce) that "condonation is upon condition of good behavior"? Is it a fiction to say that there is an "implied condition" in a will that the devisee shall not take if he kills the testator? Are "implied conditions" generally fictions?

It has already been shown how fictions "die" through a process of a change in word meanings. This quite frequently, perhaps typically, takes place through a shift of connotation from facts to legal relations. "Constructive fraud" started as a pretended actual fraud; to say today that a transaction is affected with "constructive fraud" is usually simply to affirm that it is voidable for reasons other than actual fraud—the expression relates not to pretended facts but to legal consequences. The "constructive trust" originally involved a pretense that the facts which create an actual trust were present. Today it is simply a way of stating that the case is a proper one for equitable relief.

But it should not be forgotten that the impulse to keep the form of the law persuasive—the effects of which have been traced above—is also active here. A statement of fact, even of pretended fact, will often seem—from this point of view— preferable. The case of the word "offer" will serve as an example. A offers to sell his horse to B. The "offer" remains open until A withdraws it, or until the lapse of a reasonable time. No fiction is involved in this statement; it is clear that the word "offer" here is a description of the legal situation of the parties—a situation that may be described in other language by saying that B has a "power of acceptance" which continues until something happens to destroy it. But the courts have not always been content to let the matter rest here. They have occasionally added the flourish that in legal contemplation the offer "is repeated during every moment from the time it leaves the offeror until revocation or acceptance."[60] This spoils the whole thing. An "offer" that is "repeated" must be a fact, not a legal relation. And its "repetition" is an obvious fabrication.

Legal Relations Described Metaphorically or Inadequately

Some of the hoariest of our fictions are statements that have been made by courts and that plainly refer, not to facts, but to legal relations. The fiction that "husband and wife are one"—which so puzzled Austin that he could only explain it as an expression of "sheer imbecility"[61]—is an outstanding example. But *is* this a fiction? It is a statement not of fact but of the legal situation of the parties. It is further a statement made by a court possessed of the power to create and enforce rights. If a court actually treats husband and wife as if they were one, are they not legally "one"? But it is just at this point that the fictitious element of the statement becomes apparent. The courts did not, in actuality, treat husband and wife as "one." The statement was misleading as a description of their legal situation. A legal relation, *accurately described* and *actually enforced,* cannot, with utility, be regarded as a fiction. But a description of an existing and enforced legal relation can be so inadequate and misleading as to deserve the term fiction.

"Equity regards that as done which ought to be done." "The law often regards money as land and land as money."[62]

[60] See the note "Communication of Revocation," in *18 Harv. L. Rev.* (1904), 139, 140.

[61] *Lectures on Jurisprudence* (5th ed., 1885), II, 611: "I rather impute such fictions to the sheer imbecility (or, if you will, to the active and sportive fancies) of their grave and venerable authors, than to any deliberate design, good or evil."

[62] *McIntosh* v. *Aubrey* (1902) 185 U.S. 122, 125. French jurists tend to treat what they call "real subrogation" (which seems to involve a notion similar to that involved in our "equitable conversion," i.e., the substitution of one thing for another, or, more accurately, the attribu-

Happily such "short, dark maxims" are not so common as they once were. When they are used today, it is for the sake of their flavor of antiquity, rather than because of any notion that they are actually explanatory. Undeveloped systems of law have a decided penchant for such brocards. For example, in the jurisprudential language of a tribe in east Africa, the statement "woman is a hyena" is intended as an expression of the notion of woman's legal incapacity.[63]

It is important to realize, however, that statements of this kind differ in degree but not in kind from the methods we commonly employ in describing legal relations. The legal situation that results from even the simplest sort of legal transaction is always too complicated for complete and adequate expression in a single sentence or phrase. The statement, "Husband and wife are one," does not differ in essence or purpose from the statement "A has a legal right against B to payment of $100." Both are somewhat imperfect attempts to describe a complex reality. When I am told that A has a "right" to $100 I am not informed whether A may forcibly take $100 from B's pocket, or whether A may have B jailed if B refuses to pay the $100. For the particulars I must go elsewhere. A good deal of the education of the lawyer consists in finding out in more detail what this "right" really consists of. Nor does every "right" have the same consequences. If A's action has been barred by the statute of limitations, his legal situation has been greatly altered; but he still has a "right."[64] If, on the other hand, A gets a judgment

---

tion of legal qualities usually attached to one kind of property to another kind of property) as a fiction. Lecocq, pp. 36–47. And see sec. 1407 of the French Civil Code.

[63] Post, *Grundlagen des Rechts* (1884), p. 161.

[64] This is, at least, the opinion of Professor Kocourek, "A Comment on Moral Consideration and the Statute of Limitations," *18 Ill. L. Rev.* (1924), 538. In Professor Kocourek's newer terminology, the claim descends from the zygnomic to the mesonomic plane on the running of the Statute. *Jural Relations* (1927), p. 141.

against B, his legal situation has been decidedly improved; yet the metaphysical core of his relation—however it may be garnished with new privileges, powers, and immunities—remains only a "right."[65]

The term "right" represents a rather inadequate attempt to describe a complex reality.[66] Yet this inadequacy is not regarded as unusual; one feels simply that in this case we have an illustration of the inadequacy of all expression. I am no more justified in expecting that the word "right" should tell me the detailed story of the relation of the parties than I would be in expecting that the word "house" should inform me whether the structure in question was large or small, how many doors and windows it had, etc. On the other hand, the statement "Husband and wife are one" involves an unnecessary and aberrational obscurity.[67]

Many common statements stand in a kind of twilight zone between adequacy and inadequacy, i.e., between striking or unusual inadequacy and ordinary and therefore nonapparent inadequacy. The following list might be greatly expanded: "The relation between the mortgagee and the mortgagor in possession is that of landlord and tenant." "Subrogation is an assignment." "When the mortgagor conveys the equity of redemption, promising to discharge the land of the mortgage lien, the land becomes surety for the debt." "Each joint tenant is owner of the whole." "An enforceable contract for

[65] Hohfeld, *Fundamental Legal Conceptions* (1923), p. 108.

[66] In speaking of the common reproach that the fiction does not indicate the limits of its application, Demogue (in *Les notions fondamentales du droit privé*, 1911, p. 243) says, "But may the same reproach not be directed against every formula of a technical character? Is there any difference between the formula of the fiction and any other rule of law which does not make apparent at the first glance its armature of interests to be satisfied in a certain order, as for example ... the rule that possession of personal property is equivalent to title?"

[67] Should we, following Professor Underhill Moore, call this "noninstitutional obscurity"?

the sale of land makes the vendor trustee of the land and the
vendee trustee of the purchase price."

The Form of the Fiction; Assertive and Assumptive Fictions

Gray said that the fictions of the English common law were
more "brutal" than those of the Roman law.[68] By this he did
not mean that the English fictions did more violence to the
truth than those of the Roman law—the Roman fictions were
not lacking in a certain audacity or "brutality" in that respect;
he referred to the form of the fiction.

> Fictions have played an important part in the adminis-
> tration of the Law in England, and it is characteristic of
> the two peoples that the use of fictions in England was
> bolder and, if one may say so, more brutal in England than
> it was in Rome.
> Thus, for instance, in Rome the fiction that a foreigner
> was to be considered as a citizen was applied in this way.
> It was not directly alleged that the foreigner was a citizen,
> but the mandate by the praetor to the judge who tried the
> case was put in the following form: "If, in case Aulus had
> been a Roman citizen, such a judgment ought to have been
> rendered, then render such a judgment." In England the
> plaintiff alleged a fact which was false, and the courts did
> not allow the defendant to contradict it.[69]

The Roman fiction, in other words, carried a grammatical
acknowledgment of its falsity; the English fiction appeared
as a statement of fact; its fictitious character was apparent
only to the initiate. The Roman fiction was an assumptive
fiction, a fiction taking an "as if" form; the English fiction was
(and is) a fiction ordinarily taking an "is" or assertive form.[70]

[68] Gray, *Nature and Sources of the Law* (2d ed., 1921), p. 31.
[69] *Ibid.* Gray here refers of course to the fiction that takes the form
of a procedural pretense. The conception of the fiction underlying this
article does not confine the term "fiction" to such pretenses, but would
extend it to statements made by courts in their opinions that are not
based on the pleadings.
[70] It is interesting in this connection to consider the old practice of
laying venue under a *videlicit,* in which the pleading would take some

It might seem at first glance that we were dealing here with something very fundamental. Indeed, it might be argued that an assumptive fiction (and "as if" fiction) is not a fiction at all. If a court only says that it is dealing with A *as if it were B,* it has stated nothing contrary to the fact.

Yet a closer examination will show that the distinction is one of form merely. The "supposing that" or "as if" construction in the assumptive fiction only constitutes a grammatical concession of that which is known anyway, namely, that the statement is false. When we are dealing with statements that are known to be false, it is a matter of indifference whether the author adopts a grammatical construction that concedes this falsity, or makes his statement in the form of a statement of fact.

The peculiar force that the fiction has in rendering easier alterations in the law by appeasing the longing for an appearance of conservatism seems not to be lost by clothing it in the "as if" form. The Roman praetor apparently felt that by framing his innovations in terms of older rules he had secured some justification for them, even though the pretenses involved carried on their face the acknowledgment of their falsity.

Gray apparently saw in this difference in the form of the fiction in Rome and in England some expression of a fundamental contrast in the characteristics of the two peoples. It seems likely, however, that there is a more prosaic explanation for the difference. The dissimilarity of the modes of trial in the two systems of law seems adequate to explain the diversity in the form of the fiction.[71]

---

such form as this: "on the high seas . . . 'to wit in London in the ward of Cheap.'" See Scott, *Fundamentals of Procedure in Actions at Law* (1922), p. 21. Here we have a fiction which *grammatically* takes an assertive form, and yet which, by its very context, carries as clear an admission of falsity as any grammatical sign could give it.

[71] In the Roman procedure (at the time when the praetorian fiction played its role) the actual trial of a suit was before a judge, or judex, on the basis of a written statement of the case previously drawn up by

Legal Institutions as Fictions

The oldest and most essential ideas are nearly all, if not all, fictitious. Marriage is a fictitious purchase and sale, the power of a father is a fictitious master's power, adoption is a fictitious fatherhood, in certain respects the last will and testament is (at least sometimes is) a fictitious adoption, legitimation assumes fictitiously a marriage which never existed, etc. It would not therefore be inaccurate to claim that our reality is simply fiction differentiated, and that at bottom all law is reduced to a series of fictions heaped one upon another in successive layers.[72]

Although this passage reveals a certain philosophic insight, it invites an inference that is exceedingly misleading, namely, that legal institutions may be fictitious. By legal "institutions" I mean the social effects of a legal doctrine as contrasted with the doctrine itself. Thus we may distinguish between the action of trover as an "institution" (the fact of social life that courts take certain action in certain cases) and the intellectual superstructure of this institution, the collection of legal constructions and fictions that courts developed to rationalize and explain their action. The reality of a legal institution, understood in this sense, is in no wise affected by the fact that it may be convenient to describe the institution linguistically in fictitious terms (as in the case of adoption), or by the fact that the institution may have originated historically in the

---

the praetor. Had the praetor phrased the fiction in the form of a statement of fact, it would seem likely that this would have produced confusion in the trial before the judex, which took place out of the presence of the praetor. How would the judex have known that the fact alleged was fictitious and was not to be taken seriously if the fiction had not assumed a grammatical form that warned of its falsity? On the other hand, in the English system there was always present at the trial an initiate into the freemasonry of the fiction—the judge, who was able, through proper instructions, to prevent the jury's being misled by the allegations in the pleadings.

[72] Tourtoulon, p. 387.

application of some familiar notion to a new purpose (as in the case of the marriage ceremony).[73]

Maine speaks of adoption as being one of the most important and helpful of fictions, without telling us what is fictitious about adoption.[74] The social and legal institution of adoption is not a fiction in any ordinary sense. If there is any fiction involved in the idea of adoption, it is in one of the following notions. (1) It is convenient to describe the institution by saying that the adopted child is treated *as if he were* a natural child. But this is a mere convenience of linguistic expression. (2) In primitive society adoption as a social institution probably would not have been possible without some presense of blood relationship. This is illustrated in the ceremonies that accompany adoption in primitive society, as where the child is dropped through the clothing of the adopting parent in imitation of birth.[75] (3) The original invention of the notion of adoption involved, probably, an imaginative flight, an exercise of ingenuity, similar to that which attends the birth of a legal fiction. But none of these

[73] Upon a somewhat deeper level of discourse, a social or legal institution may be regarded as a fiction in the sense in which the word "fiction" is used by Vaihinger. In fact (or at least "in fact" if one does not penetrate to a still deeper plane of discourse) we have only an enormous number of individual acts by individual human beings, never taking quite the same form and never having quite the same purpose. To introduce simplicity into a welter of individual actions, we postulate certain "institutions," we group together certain recurring acts which show a thread of similarity into a conceptual entity which we call an institution. A later age may classify our actions upon an entirely different basis than that we are accustomed to, may see in our conduct a different set of "institutions." Conversely, our classification of our own actions into "institutions" may seem as arbitrary and unreal to a later age as the concept of "seisin" seems arbitrary and unreal to the modern student of law.

[74] Maine, p. 26.

[75] Hamilton-Grierson, "An Example of Legal Make-Believe," *20 Juridical Rev.* (1908), 32, and *21* (1909), 17. Strangely enough, the ceremony of dropping the child through the clothing is performed even when the adopting person is a man.

facts means that adoption, as a social institution existing in present-day society, is a fiction.

One should also guard against the converse sort of error, that of supposing that because there is a social reality back of a fictitious statement, the statement itself is therefore non-fictitious. Professor Sturm protests that the quasi-contract is not a fiction because it represents a social institution, that in such-and-such cases recovery may be had in the courts.[76] But this does not keep the *term* quasi-contract ("as if" contract) from being fictional. If it is not felt as a fiction, the reason lies in the fact that it is not regarded as containing an element of pretense; it is, in the terminology established earlier in this article, a dead fiction, a term of classification and analysis, merely.

Fictions and Legal Presumptions

A distinction commonly taken between the fiction and the legal presumption runs somewhat as follows: A fiction assumes something that is known to be false; a presumption (whether conclusive or rebuttable) assumes something that may possibly be true.[77] This distinction is regarded as being reinforced, as it were, in the case of the rebuttable presumption because such a presumption assumes a fact that *probably* is true.

How valid is this distinction? And—what is more important—how significant is it, assuming that it states at least a partial truth? In attempting an answer to these questions it will be convenient to start with the conclusive presumption.

Now in the first place it is fairly clear, I think, that the conclusive presumption is generally applied in precisely those

[76] Sturm, *Fiktion und Vergleich in der Rechtswissenschaft* (1915), p. 47.
[77] Best, *A Treatise on Presumptions of Law and Fact* (1844), sec. 20; Lecocq, p. 29.

cases where the fact assumed is false and is known to be false. For example, there is said to be a presumption that the grantee of a gift has accepted it.[78] In practice the only cases in which this presumption is invoked are cases where the grantee did not know of the gift and hence could not possibly have "accepted" it. Hence, the statement that a conclusive presumption assumes a fact which may be true is at least misleading, in that it ignores the circumstance that the occasion to use the conclusive presumption generally arises precisely in those cases where the fact is known to be false. When the fact is present it may usually be proved, and there is no occasion for the presumption.

But this is not always so. Conceivably, the presumed fact may be present in reality in a case where the party chooses to rely on the conclusive presumption, either because proof would be difficult or because he does not know whether the fact is present or not.[79] In such a case does the application of the presumption involve any fiction? I think that it does.

A conclusive presumption is not a fiction because the fact assumed is false, for in that event it would cease to be a fiction if the fact happened to be true.[80] The ordinary fiction simply says, "Fact A is present" and would cease to be a fiction if Fact A were in reality present in the case. But the conclusive presumption says, "The presence of Fact X is conclusive proof of Fact A." This statement is false, since we know that

---

[78] *Thompson* v. *Leach* (1690) 2 Vent. 198.

[79] The presumption of "fraudulent intent" on the part of one who has given away his property while insolvent might be invoked by a creditor in a case in which the debtor actually did make the conveyance for the purpose of evading the claims of his creditors.

[80] Lecocq, at p. 29, contains a remarkable bit of reasoning. He says it might seem that we ought to say the presumption is a fiction when the fact assumed is false, and not a fiction when the assumed fact is true. But, he says, this would involve an error, because it would be "anti-juridical" to inquire whether the fact is true or not because the presumption is set up for the express purpose of avoiding that inquiry!

Fact X does not "conclusively prove" Fact A. And this statement, that Fact X proves the existence of Fact A, remains
false, even though Fact A may by chance be present in a
particular case.[81] The conclusive presumption attributes to
the facts "an artificial effect beyond their natural tendency to
produce belief."[82] It "attaches to any given possibility a degree of certainty to which it normally has no right. It know-
ingly gives an insufficient proof the value of a sufficient
one."[83]

But what of the rebuttable presumption? Can it clear itself
of the charge of being fictitious?

In the first place, it should be noted that the difference between the rebuttable presumption and the conclusive presumption may, in some cases, become a matter of degree.
Some of our rebuttable presumptions have, in the course of
time, gathered about them rules declaring what is sufficient
to overcome them. As soon as you have begun to limit and
classify those things that will rebut a presumption, you are
importing into the facts "an arbitrary effect" beyond their natural tendency to produce belief. No presumption can be
wholly nonfictitious that is not "freely" rebuttable. To the
extent that rebuttal is limited, the *prima facie* or rebuttable
presumption has the same effect as a conclusive presumption.

In the second place, it is clear that a rebuttable presumption will be regarded as establishing a fiction if we feel that
the inference that underlies it is not supported by common
experience. Some courts have applied a *prima facie* presump-

[81] A creditor sets aside a gift made by his debtor while insolvent.
Now, even though the fact is that the debtor actually intended to de-
fraud his creditor in making the conveyance, the pretense involved in
the presumption—that this fact is conclusively proved by the circumstance that he was giving away his property while insolvent—remains
false.

[82] Best, p. 19.

[83] Tourtoulon, p. 398. Tourtoulon would regard this statement as
applying also to the rebuttable presumption.

tion that, where a child is injured or killed in the streets, the parents must be considered as having been guilty of negligence.[84] Now, even though this presumption may be rebutted by any pertinent evidence, most of us would not hesitate to say that it contains an element of fiction. We do not feel that the inference it establishes is justified by ordinary experience.

If, therefore, we are to have any hope of escaping fiction in a discussion of presumptions we must narrow our inquiry to the case of the presumption that is freely rebuttable and that establishes an inference justified by ordinary experience. There is a presumption that a deed in the possession of the grantee has been delivered.[85] The presumption is freely rebuttable; any pertinent evidence may be considered as overcoming it. Furthermore, it may be argued, the presumption establishes an inference that experience and common sense justify; it is based on the fact of social life that deeds in the hands of grantees usually have been delivered. Does such a presumption involve any fiction?

But first it will be legitimate to inquire, if the presumption is so reasonable and so much a matter of common sense, might it not be safe to assume that the judge or jury would have made exactly the same inference without the presumption? In other words, is a presumption that merely states a proposition of common sense a significant rule of law? Does it really affect the administration of justice?

It may be urged in answer to these inquiries that that which seems "reasonable" and a "mere matter of common sense" to the author of the presumption may not seem so to the agency (the judge or the jury) which applies the presumption. It may be urged that the function of the sort of presumption we are here considering is simply to prevent the judge or jury from departing from the ordinary principles of ratiocination.

[84] 75 U.P. Law Rev. (1927), 476.
[85] Tiffany, II, 1750.

The law is as much concerned that its agencies shall follow common sense in deciding disputes as it is that they shall apply legal doctrine correctly. And the presumption may be simply a way of ensuring the application of common sense.

If we regard a particular presumption in this light—and I think, incidentally, that the number of those that are entitled to be so regarded is small—then it must be admitted that the presumption would involve no fiction were it not for the fact that we habitually treat the presumption, not as directing a disposition of the case, but as "directing an inference" or as commanding an "act of reasoning."[86] Now the presumption may have been the product of a process of inference on the part of the one originally conceiving it. But if the presumption is treated by the judge and jury as a rule of law, it is clear that it is not an "inference" as to them. If I am merely accepting someone else's ready-made inference, I am not "inferring." There is then a fiction in the case of any rebuttable presumption in the sense that we ordinarily treat as an "inference" what is in reality passive acceptance of an imposed

[86] Abbott, C. J., in *Rex* v. *Burdett* (1820) 4 B. & Ald. 161: "A presumption of any fact is, properly, an inferring of that fact from other facts that are known; it is an act of reasoning." In Wigmore on *Evidence* (2d ed., 1923), V, sec. 2491, the view is taken that a presumption is not an "inference" but merely a rule "attaching to one evidentiary fact certain procedural consequences as to the duty of production of other evidence by the opponent." This, as Dean Wigmore's own remarks show, is intended as a statement of how we *ought* to regard the presumption, rather than as a factual description of how it is commonly regarded by the profession.

It might be remarked parenthetically that a complete discussion of the presumption would have to distinguish presumptions according to the manner in which they are applied. Some presumptions simply operate to "shift the burden of proof." In some jurisdictions the same presumptions that "shift the burden of proof" are also presented to the jury as having a probative force to be considered along with the other evidence of the case (Wigmore, *Evidence*, p. 452, n. 5). Some presumptions are not applied procedurally at all, but are only intended, apparently, as somewhat cryptic statements of a general principle, as the presumption that every man "intends the normal consequences of his acts." I have attempted to make my remarks sufficiently general to cover any case of the presumption, however applied.

principle. The fiction here relates, not to the subject matter of the presumption, but to its effect in the administration of justice.

These points may perhaps be made clearer by a simile. We may treat the presumption as a lens held before the facts of reality. Now if the lens produces a *distortion* of reality—as in the case of the presumption of negligence where a child is injured in the streets—we do not hesitate to attribute a fictional character to the image produced. On the other hand, we may be convinced that a particular lens produces a *true* image of nature. Now if we are willing to attribute to the judge or jury normal vision (ordinary powers of ratiocination), does it not follow that if our lens gives a true picture of reality it must in fact be of plain glass, i.e., produce no alteration at all? On the other hand, if we conceive of our lens as a *corrective* device— if we recognize that we are curing a defect—then there is no fiction *if we recognize that we are changing the image*. But our professional linguistic habits tend to keep us in the paradoxical position of insisting that the lens *does not change anything* and at the same time of asserting that it is *necessary*— that without it a different result might be reached. We tend to assume, not that we have corrected the vision of the judge or jury by artificial means, but that by a kind of legal miracle we have given normal sight to the astigmatic. We tend to assume what unfortunately cannot be—that the law has a "mandamus to the logical faculty."[87]

A presumption, if it is to escape the charge of "fiction," must, then, comply with at least three requirements: (1) be based on an inference justified by common experience, (2) be freely rebuttable, (3) be phrased in realistic terms; order, not an "inference," but a disposition of the case in a certain contingency.

---

[87] Thayer, p. 314, note. "The law has no mandamus to the logical faculty; it orders nobody to draw inferences—common as that mode of expression is."

Assuming that a presumption has met all of these requirements, has it established its right to be considered wholly nonfictitious? There is a presumption of death where one has
been absent, unheard from, for a period of seven years.[88] It
is possible to consider this presumption as meeting all three
of the requirements enumerated. The presumption may be regarded as based on an inference warranted by experience.
When people have been gone for seven years and have not
been heard from, *usually* they are dead. The presumption is
freely rebuttable. And it may be—though usually it is not—
phrased in nonfictitious terms, i.e., not as ordering an "inference" of death but as ordering the judge or jury to treat the
case as they would one of death. Does it follow that the presumption establishes a proposition that is wholly nonfictitious,
i.e., entirely "true"? It is apparent at once that the "truth" of
this presumption is a conventionalized, formalized truth. Why
should the period be set at exactly seven years? Why should
one disposition of a case be made when the absence is six
years and eleven months, and a different disposition be made
one month later?

This formal, arbitrary element is very conspicuous in the
presumption just mentioned. To some extent it is perhaps
inherent in all presumptions, of whatever character. A formal
rule, no matter how firmly rooted its foundations may be in
reality, tends to gather about itself a force not entirely justified by its foundations. It crystallizes and formalizes the truth
it expresses. If the presumption is given any weight at all by
the judge or jury, there is probably a tendency to give it too
much weight.[89] In the language of the figure adopted previ-

[88] Wigmore on *Evidence*, V, sec. 2531(b).
[89] This point may be illustrated by the following case. Two years
after the death of Q, X claims Blackacre under a deed now in his possession and signed by Q. The facts show that X never made any claim
to the land during the life of Q, and that after the death of Q he had
access to Q's papers. X relies on the presumption that a deed in the

ously, no lens is a perfect lens. In correcting a defect of sight, the lens produces its own peculiar distortions and that which was intended merely as a correction is usually an overcorrection. In this sense every presumption is perhaps a distortion of reality. But this fact probably does not justify the application of the term "fiction." As has been said previously, we reserve the term "fiction" for those distortions of reality that are outstanding and unusual. And the distortion produced by the formal, imperative quality of the presumption is an inevitable incident of the process of reducing a complex truth to a simple, formal statement.

The close kinship of the ordinary fiction and the presumption is shown by the fact that the two meet upon a common grammatical field in such expressions as "deemed" and "regarded as." "The testator must be deemed to have intended to attach a condition upon his gift." Does this mean, "Conceding that the testator had no such intent in fact, we feel it advisable to treat the case as if that had been his intent"? Or does it mean, "Although the evidence is not clear, we feel justified in inferring that the testator in fact intended to attach a condition on his gift"? In truth, probably the statement

---

possession of the grantee has been delivered. Do these facts "rebut" the presumption? Or—what is the same thing—do they prevent its "arising"? Now, if the judge in passing on this question is simply weighing the fact of social life, that deeds in the possession of the grantee are usually delivered, against the peculiar circumstances of this case, then he is not using the presumption at all. He is using his own reasoning powers. But if the judge is attributing a special significance to the circumstance that the above-mentioned fact of social life has been incorporated into a rule of law, then the presumption is having an "artificial effect." If the judge is saying to himself, "Deeds in the hands of grantees are usually delivered, and *I must remember that this fact has been specifically recognized by the law in a formal presumption,*" then he is dealing, to some extent, with proofs that are formal and not real. Since the question when a presumption "arises"—or, what is the same thing, when it is "rebutted"—always involves a certain discretion, it may be said that whenever the presumption has any effect at all, its effect is a formal and artificial one.

meant neither of these things—and both. That is to say, the mind of the author of this statement had not reached the state of clarification in which this distinction would become apparent. He probably would have agreed with either interpretation of his meaning. This example indicates, I think, that the mental process involved in the invention of the ordinary fiction is at least a close relation to that involved in the establishment of a presumption, and suggests the possibility that there may be a primitive undifferentiated form of thought that includes both.

2. What Motives Give Rise to the Legal Fiction?

In our first chapter an attempt was made to answer the question, what is a legal fiction? The next problem to be addressed is, why does the legal fiction exist? What motives lead courts and legal writers to employ the fiction?[1]

This inquiry will, of necessity, lead us into a conjectural field. One can scarcely conceive of a more complex and speculative problem than that of human motives. The motives that lead to a resort to fiction are as complex, as remote, and as numerous as the springs of human conduct generally. And yet, in spite of the difficulties of the inquiry, it is submitted that no truly productive classification of fictions can be made that is not based on motives. Every attempt to classify fictions on the basis of mere logical or grammatical form is doomed to sterility.[2] A fiction becomes understandable only when we

---

[1] A portion of this chapter was substantially revised and published under the title "What Motives Give Rise to the Historical Legal Fiction?" in *Recueil d'Etudes en l'honneur de François Gény* (n.d.), II, 157–76.

[2] One can find all kinds of classifications in the literature of fictions. Thus, there are fictions where the effect exceeds the cause, where the effect is produced without a cause, and where the effect precedes the cause (Lecocq, *De la fiction comme procédé juridique* [1914], p. 32); affirmative and negative fictions (Best, *A Treatise on Presumptions of Law and Fact* [1844], sec. 21); restricted and unrestricted fictions (Bernhöft, *Zur Lehre von den Fiktionen* [1907], p. 9); rhetorical, symbolic, classificatory, and analogical fictions (Mallachow, *Rechtserkenntnistheorie und Fiktionslehre* [1922], p. 29). I have attempted here to

know why it exists, and we can know that only when we know what actuated its author.

The ultimate end of our inquiry is to make possible an intelligent criticism of the worth of the fiction as a device of legal thought and expression. From this point of view it is fairly obvious that an examination of motives cannot be avoided. But even if we renounce the privilege of criticism and are interested in the fiction merely as a part of "positive law," as an expression of "law as it is," still we cannot forgo an inquiry into motives. It is essential that we know *why* courts resort to fiction if we are to understand what is meant by their fictions. One of the objections most commonly raised against the fiction is that it does not define its field of application. "Title relates back" . . . but for what purposes? In what specific situations will the fiction be applied? The scope of any particular fiction becomes defined only when we know what actuated its author. "In simple but loose words, we only know for certain *what* is said when we know *why* it is said."[3]

There are a great many maxims governing the application of fictions. "No fiction shall be allowed to work an injury."[4] "Fictions are to be strictly construed."[5] These illustrations show the general tendency of the maxims. They are all designed to prevent a gross misapplication of the fiction by one who does not understand it. When one fully grasps the purpose of a particular fiction, these general directions have no value. As Demogue has said with reference to the rule that fictions are to be narrowly interpreted, the true principle is simply that fictions are to be applied in the light of the reasons

---

make no distinctions or classifications that are not productive. To me it has seemed that the productive principle of classification is that of motives.

[3] Ogden and Richards, *The Meaning of Meaning* (2d ed., 1927), p. 94, note.

[4] Blackstone, *Commentaries on the Law of England* (Lewis ed., 1897), III, *43.

[5] Demogue, *Les notions fondamentales du droit privé* (1911), p. 246.

back of them.[6] But it is not always a simple matter to discover the purposes of a particular fiction.

A *Fiction Serves to Reconcile a Legal Result with Some Expressed or Assumed Premise*

Speaking for the moment in the most general terms, the purpose of any fiction is to reconcile a specific legal result with some premise or postulate. Where no intellectual premises are assumed, the fiction has no place. An autocrat, deciding disputes upon the basis of instinct or selfish interest and feeling no compulsion to explain his decisions, either to litigants or to himself, would have no occasion to resort to fiction. A premiseless law would be a fictionless law—if it could be called law at all. A modern writer has by his own example shown how, by eliminating the premises that are generally assumed in the law, it is possible to purge the law of fictions.[7] He defines law as "a species-preserving propensity" in man, and regards legal institutions, not as products of an articulate intellectual process, but as resting directly upon the instincts. He avoids the sophistries and contradictions to be found in most theories of punishment by simply declaring punishment to be "a psychological necessity"... *und damit Punktum!* In effect, he rejects the entire intellectual superstructure of the law, and with it all necessity for fiction—except one all-embracing fiction, that the law proceeds directly from the instincts without intellectual contamination. But most of us would not be disposed to follow his theory, particularly those of us who earn our living teaching law—for obvious reasons. But if we reject his theory, if

---

[6] *Ibid.*, n. 93. Cf. "But fictions of law hold only in respect to the ends and purposes for which they were invented; when they are urged to an intent and purpose not within the reason and policy of the fiction, the other party may show the truth." Mansfield, L.J., in *Morris* v. *Pugh* (1761) 3 Burr. 1242, 1243.

[7] Sturm, *Fiktion und Vergleich in der Rechtswissenschaft* (1915).

we conceive of the law as at least in part an intellectual product, we are at once confronted with the problem of the fiction. For the fiction is the cement that is always at hand to plaster together the weak spots in our intellectual structure.

A premiseless law would be a fictionless law; we eliminate the necessity for fiction in direct proportion as we eliminate premises from the law, as we disencumber the law of intellectualism. But this proposition has its converse. The importation of unusual premises into the law will lead one to detect fictions where no one dreamed of their existence before. Alteserra, writing in 1659, regarded slavery as founded on a fiction, because "in nature all men are equal."[8] Gray, by proceeding upon the assumption that only a being with a "will" could have legal rights, was forced to regard corporate personality as a fiction devised to escape this premise, and cut himself off from the simpler explanation that the "personality" of the corporation is only an expository figure of speech.[9] If we assume that a trial court deals only with "proofs," then we must say that matters falling within the doctrine of judicial notice are "deemed proved."[10] And so we might go through the list of all the legal fictions ever devised and show how each might be eliminated if we struck down some expressed or assumed premise. We may say, in short, that the necessity for fiction will vary directly with the number and inflexibility of the postulates assumed.

---

[8] In "De fictionibus juris," cited in Lecocq, p. 217.

[9] The fiction, as Gray saw it, consisted in the fact that the "wills" of the agents of the corporation were attributed to the corporation itself. (*Nature and Sources of the Law* [2d ed., 1921], p.50.) This was regarded by Gray as unavoidable, because, he thought, "in order that a legal right be exercised, a will is necessary, and, therefore, so far as the exercise of legal rights is concerned, a person must have a will." (*Ibid.*, p. 27.) But one will look in vain in Gray for an explanation of what is meant by a "will" and why it is that "rights" are attributable only to beings with wills.

[10] "Facts of which judicial notice is taken are *deemed proved* without any act of the parties." Fisk, "Presumptions," 11 *Cornell L. Quar.* (1925), 20, 21.

To obtain an understanding of any particular fiction we must first inquire: What premise does it assume? With what proposition is it seeking to reconcile the decision at hand? In most cases the answer is easily discovered. Generally a fiction is intended to escape the consequences of an existing, specific rule of law. Thus the fiction of "inviting" in the "attractive nuisance" cases is intended to escape the rule that there is no duty of care toward trespassers.

But occasionally the matter is more obscure. In some cases a fiction seems to be intended to avoid the implications, not of any specific and recognized rule of law, but of some unexpressed and rather general and vague principle of jurisprudence or morals. Thus, the conclusive presumption that the donee of a gift accepts the gift, although it may have been delivered out of his presence and without his knowledge, assumes a general principle that title cannot pass to a man without his assent. The conclusive presumption that everyone knows the law is, apparently, intended to escape an assumed moral principle that it is unjust to visit the legal consequences of an act upon a person who does not know the law. This very interesting fact exists in both cases—the only recognition that the assumed principle finds is in the very fiction by which it is evaded![11]

The Expository and Emotive Functions of the Fiction

In dealing with the motives for the fiction, probably the most fundamental distinction we can make is between expository and emotive fictions. The author of a fiction may have used it as a means of conveying what he had in mind; his motive may have been simply to achieve a succinct mode

---

[11] Of course, some jurisdictions refuse to follow the first of the fictions mentioned and require proof of acceptance. See, for example, *Mahoney v. Martin* (1905) 72 Kan. 406, 83 Pac. 982, and *Welch v. Sackett* (1860) 12 Wis. 243. But the statement in the text remains true in those jurisdictions that embrace the fiction.

of expression. On the other hand, the author of a fiction may employ it for other—we are tempted to say, less worthy— purposes. He may prefer a pretense to a plain statement of fact because of the emotive force of the pretense.

Of course the same distinction exists in the case of the ordinary metaphor of literature. For example, the complicated psychological process of habit formation may be described by saying that the repetition of a reaction "cuts a groove" in the nervous system. Here the purpose of the metaphor is expository merely; it is a "convenient shorthand." But a metaphor may be used for the sake of its emotive power, as when the suggestion of government operation of the liquor industry is described as a proposal "to put a beer towel over Uncle Sam's arm." And so it is with the legal fiction, with the difference that the emotive legal fiction is, invariably I think, a *persuasive* device. There seem to be no legal fictions designed to dissuade from a course of conduct; the emotive legal fiction seems to be intended rather to induce conviction that a given legal result is just and proper. We may therefore call emotive legal fictions "persuasive fictions," bearing always in mind that the author of the fiction may be as much influenced by its persuasive power as his audience.

It should not be assumed that every fiction is either of the one type or of the other, or that every fiction is always used and understood in the same manner. It has already been pointed out how some fictions waver between a purely expository and a persuasive function.[12] A fiction that was originally intended to persuade may later be retained for its expository power. The statement "A corporation is a person" may have had at times a political purpose;[13] yet this does not

[12] See the discussion of "constructive notice" in Chapter 1, pp. 24–26.
[13] Dewey, "Corporate Legal Personality," 35 *Yale L. Jour.* (1926), 655, 664, n. 11. "One potent recent motive for the insistence upon the real 'personality' of social groups, or corporate bodies, independent of

seriously impair its utility as an expository device. Conceivably a fiction intended by its author merely as a convenient mode of expression may have an unanticipated persuasive effect upon the hearer. Every teacher of property law knows how difficult it is to convince students that the only proper function of the "relation back" of title is as a device of expression.

In the last section it was stated that the purpose of any fiction is to reconcile a specific legal result with some premise. This is true, at least in form, of both the expository and persuasive types. The expository fiction of corporate personality serves to preserve the premise that only "persons" can have rights. The persuasive fiction of the "acceptance" of a gift delivered out of the presence of the donee operates to keep intact the assumed notion that no one can secure a title without an expression of his will. The difference, however, lies in motives. The expository fiction of corporate personality preserves the premise that only "persons" have rights in order to avoid the circumlocution that would otherwise be necessary. The persuasive fiction of "acceptance" is designed to make it appear that the postulate assumed has in fact not been departed from. In the case of the expository fiction, because of the linguistic change that almost inevitably occurs,[14] the reconciliation of the specific result with a premise takes place *in form* only; in fact, the premise is altered (the word "person" acquires a new meaning) to fit the specific result. In the case

---

the state, is opposition to the claim that the state is the sole or even supreme Person." And even the theory that corporate personality is a mere fiction, a figure of speech, was advanced in the Middle Ages with a political purpose: "The doctrine was stated as the reason why an ecclesiastic *collegium* or *universitas,* or *capitulum* could not be excommunicated, or be guilty of a delict." (Dewey, *ibid.,* p. 665.) One could not excommunicate a mere name, or hold a name responsible for a misdeed.

[14] See the discussion of "live" and "dead" fictions in Chapter 1, p. 14ff.

of the persuasive fiction this linguistic change ordinarily does not take place,[15] because when it has occurred, the reason for the fiction ceases to exist.

Historical and Nonhistorical Fictions

A given fiction may or may not have had for its original purpose the introduction of a change into the law. Many of our fictions—probably most of the fictions of the English common law—had this purpose in the beginning. As to many of them, we know, or can discover, the details of their creation, what rule they were designed to escape, what specific change resulted from their application, "who devised them and how the exigencies of meeting a special case where existing legal materials were inadequate moved him to do so."[16] These are the historical fictions dealt with so penetratingly by Maine.[17]

But not all of our fictions have a historic or "creative" function. Many of them, as will be shown later, are intended merely as expositions of the law "as it is"; some few may perhaps be intended as apologies for rules of law that have existed from the beginning of our legal system.

The Motives for the Historical Fiction

We turn now to a more particular examination of the motives back of the historical fiction. Why do courts so frequently introduce new law in the guise of old? What impulses have produced this habit of mind? Speaking in general terms, one may say, of course, that the impulse is one of conservatism. But "conservatism," after all, is only a description of a tendency, not an explanation for it. What is

[15] But there are important exceptions, as in the case of "constructive possession," "constructive fraud," "implied malice," etc. See pp. 18–19, 22–23.

[16] Pound, *Interpretations of Legal History* (1923), p. 130.

[17] *Ancient Law* (1861; Beacon Press ed., 1963), ch. II.

back of this conservatism? A closer examination of the problem will reveal that a number of distinct motives may be segregated. In the discussion that follows, an attempt is made to distinguish the *conservatism of policy, emotional conservatism,* the *conservatism of convenience,* and, last, what will be called for want of a better term *intellectual conservatism.* We shall begin with the least worthy of these.

The motive of policy. There was no doubt in Bentham's mind about the purpose of the historical fiction. It was "a wilful falsehood, having for its object the stealing of legislative power, by and for hands which could not, or durst not, openly claim it, and but for the delusion thus produced could not exercise it."[18] Austin recognizes that the motive may be "a wish to conciliate (as far as possible) the friends or lovers of the law which they [the judges] really annulled. If a praetor, or other subordinate judge, had said openly and avowedly, 'I abrogate such a law,' or 'I make such a law,' he might have given offence to the lovers of things ancient, by his direct and arrogant assumption of legislative power. By covering the innovation with a decent lie, he treated the abrogated law with all seemly respect, whilst he knocked it on the head."[19] In short, a judge, fully conscious that he is changing the law, chooses, for reasons of policy, to deceive others into believing that he is merely applying existing law.

It cannot be positively affirmed that Bentham and Austin were wrong; it cannot be proved that courts may not, in some instances, have employed fictions with a deliberate intention of deceiving the public. But most of us would feel that this interpretation is somewhat uncharitable to the courts. In the first place, it is a little difficult to see how the supposed deceit could actually succeed. Bentham and Austin were not fooled

---

[18] *Works* (J. Bowring's ed., 1843), p. 243. Cf. "The fiction is frequently resorted to in the attempt to conceal the fact that the law is undergoing alteration at the hands of the judges." J. Smith, "Surviving Fictions," 27 *Yale L. Jour.* (1917), 147, 150.

[19] *Lectures on Jurisprudence* (5th ed., 1885), II, 610.

by it. Is it likely that anyone who knew the facts, i.e., what the preexisting law was and what the fiction accomplished, could be deluded?

It is true that the fiction may *obscure* the process of legislating. Without deceiving anyone into the belief that no change has occurred in the law, it may serve to create the impression that the change is no greater than that involved in the ordinary case where legal principles are extended by way of analogy. It may temper the boldness of the change. But inasmuch as it does this, the fiction probably has as much effect on the judge employing it as on his audience. And this brings us to a consideration of emotional conservatism.

Emotional conservatism. A judge may state new law in the guise of old, not for the purpose of deceiving others, but because this form of statement satisfies his own longing for a feeling of conservatism and certainty. As a famous judge himself has said, speaking on behalf of his profession, "We may think the law is the same if we refuse to change the formulas."[20] And presumably this feeling that the law "is the same" and that existing law determines the case at hand is a comforting one for the man whose business consists in a regular intervention in the affairs of his fellow citizens.

I call this the motive of emotional conservatism because it proceeds, not from any clearly formulated theory of the process of law making, but from an emotional and obscurely felt judgment that stability is so precious a thing that even the *form* of stability, its empty shadow, has a value.

The conservatism of policy, discussed in the last section, proceeds presumably from a conscious intent to deceive *others;* it involves an external deception. Emotional conservatism, on the other hand, involves a process of *internal* deception, of self-deception.

This is the motive commonly attributed to the courts that

---

[20] Cardozo, *The Paradoxes of Legal Science* (1928), p. 11.

developed the fictions of the English common law, and to the praetor in Rome. Austin recognizes it when he says that the fiction may be produced by "a respect on the part of the innovating judges for the law which they virtually changed."[21] Strangely enough, this motive is not recognized by the two most famous Romanists, Savigny and Ihering. They apparently recognize only the motive of convenience.

The motive of convenience. Ihering regarded the following brief account of the legal fiction by Savigny as "exhausting its true nature":

> When a new juridical form arises it is joined directly on to an old and existing institution and in this way the certainty and development of the old is procured for the new. This is the notion of the Fiction, which was of the greatest importance in the development of the Roman Law and which has often been laughably misunderstood by moderns ... And because in this way legal thinking progresses from simplicity to the most variegated development, steadily and without external disturbance or interruption, the Roman jurists were able to attain, even in later times, that complete mastery of their subject which we admire in them.[22]

Ihering's own discussion of the fiction begins with a reference to the passage from Savigny quoted above and then proceeds:

> To be sure the fiction presents a certain temptation to this "laughable misunderstanding." It is one of the phenomena of legal technique by means of which it is easy to make Roman jurisprudence seem ridiculous to the uninitiated ... How puerile it is, one may say, simply to *imagine away* a legal difficulty one cannot solve; to sweep aside the prejudicial effects of an emancipation by declaring it not to have

---

[21] *Lectures on Jurisprudence,* II, 609.
[22] Savigny, *Vom Beruf unserer Zeit für Gesetzgebung und Rechtswissenschaft* (2d ed., 1828), pp. 32–33.

happened; to make the daughter of the patron a son, the foreigner a citizen; and even to confer children on the chaste Diana in order to procure for her the capacity for inheritance attached to the jus liberorum. How indeed lawyers could let themselves be deceived by the whimsical device of the fiction is hard to understand, and yet literary history presents a striking example in one of the most renowned of the jurists of the last century [Heineccius].

And yet the thing is so remarkably simple! I may perhaps be allowed to use as an illustration an example from modern life. The administration of a railway or a taxing board has had schedules printed in which, through inadvertence or because the article was not at the time known, a column or heading for an article—which, let us say, in the interim has become common—is lacking. In order to avoid the necessity of reprinting the whole schedule they provide that the article shall be brought under one of the existing columns; that lignite, for example, shall be regarded as hard coal. Did the praetor do anything different when he extended actions to new situations and preserved the old formulas unchanged, simply adding the remark for the judex that he should treat the new situation as if it fell in the category of the old? It was, in fact, nothing but a peculiar form of the analogical extension of the law.

This and no other purpose has the fiction. It is intended to save the praetor the trouble of altering the formulation of the action, and legal theory the trouble of altering the concept. "Only an heir can bring the hereditatis petitio"— thus ran the provision of the old law. But later the necessity arose to grant the action to other persons; for example, to the purchaser of a bankrupt estate and to the bonorum possessor. In consequence of that it would have been necessary to change, not simply the wording of the *action* (which spoke in terms of the heres or hereditas), but also the formulation of the above *rule*. This last was not easy. It meant, in place of the current, familiar notion of the hereditas, substituting a new, more general notion, that of universal succession, which would have to be clearly conceived and formulated. Should life wait until legal theory had succeeded in this? A way was chosen which was theoretically less correct but which in practice reached the goal more quickly; those two persons [the bonorum emptor and the bonorum possessor] are regarded as heredes. They are not heredes of course, but are feigned, i.e., treated, as such; in this particular situation they are placed on an equality with heredes. In this way the form of the existing law was saved. The praetor still issued the same formula as before, with the addition only of the remark [for the judex] mentioned above; the teacher of law expounded the same rule as before and answered the objection of the student (that these persons were after all not heredes) in the same way that the praetor answered the possible doubt of the judex— although in fact these persons were not heredes, they were with respect to the capacity for bringing an action placed on an equality with heredes; the right of action of the heres had been carried over to them.

"The testament is the last will of a Roman citizen; whoever lacks this status at the time of his death can leave no valid testament." This was the principle of the old law. As a consequence of this the testament of a citizen who died in the captivity of the enemy had no validity [since captivity involved a loss of citizenship]. The lex Cornelia abrogated this consequence insofar as it applied to a testament made before captivity. This might have been done in the way in which we would do it today; i.e., this reform might have been openly declared. It probably would have been done in that way, too, had not the Roman lawyers taken part in the deliberations and preserved the interests of their discipline by devising an expedient that preserved the external form of the above-mentioned principle—the well-known fictio legis Corneliae. The statute declared that the case should be regarded as if the testator had died at the instant he was taken prisoner, while he was still a free man and a Roman citizen.

These two illustrations will be sufficient to show the peculiar mechanism and the technical purpose of the fiction.

The purpose of the fiction consists in making lighter the difficulties connected with the assimilation and elaboration of new, more or less revolutionary, legal principles; in making it possible to leave the traditional learning in its old form, yet without hindering thereby the practical efficiency of the new in any way . . . It is therefore not accident, but a sound instinct, that bids Science in her infancy take up these crutches; and once again the example of the English law (which has made a most extended application of this expedient) can teach us that we are dealing here, not with a device that is peculiarly Roman, but with something that, at a certain stage of legal development, crops out of an inner compulsion. And even when Science has outgrown her swaddling clothes and centuries of mental discipline have matured in her that certainty and dexterity in abstract thought which the reorganization of the foundations of a system demands, still the fiction can have a certain justification as the first step toward the mastery of a new thought, in a situation of theoretic necessity. Better order and easy mobility with the fiction, than disorder and stagnation without it![23]

Despite the fact that Ihering begins with the assertion that the matter is extremely simple, his own point of view seems to undergo a discernible alteration in the course of his discussion. The statement toward the end of this quotation, that the fiction is often the "first step toward the mastery of a new thought," is a long way from his simile of the railway board. Certainly no railway board ever found it necessary to think of lignite as hard coal in order to conceive of its being subject to the same tariff as hard coal!

But let us, for the moment, concentrate our attention on the point of view expressed in the first parts of this discussion. Here Ihering seems to contemplate a judge or legislator who wishes to change the law and who knows exactly *why* he wishes to change it and precisely *what* reform he desires to achieve. He could, if he chose, state the new rule accurately and completely in nonfictitious language. But he chooses to employ a fiction that brings the reform within the linguistic cover of existing law. Why? Simply because this will avoid discommoding current notions. Change always carries with it

[23] Ihering, *Geist des römischen Rechts* (6th ed.; 1923), III[1], 301–6.

troublesome adjustments to the new situation. Let us, therefore, restrict the reform to as narrow limits as possible; let it affect the substance but not the form of existing law. In this way existing treatises will not have to be rewritten—if one reads judiciously between the lines, everything now stated in them remains true. Lawyers will not have to change their concepts—they need only change the content of these concepts. This seems to be the point of view expressed in the first part of Ihering's discussion.

Is it really ever convenient to cover a reform with a pretense where the judge is able to state it in nonfictitious terms? Did the Roman jurists really "preserve the interests of their discipline" by making a statute (which could have provided simply that captivity did not abrogate a will) take the awkward form of stating that the testator should be deemed to have died at the moment of his captivity?[24] Is it true, as Savigny says, that the Roman lawyers were able to "attain that complete mastery of their subject which we admire in them" because the Roman law was honeycombed with fictions? With all deference to such eminent authority, it seems exceedingly questionable whether it is ever truly convenient to employ a fiction where the judge introducing the reform can state the new rule in nonfictitious terms.

But suppose the judge finds that he *cannot* state the reform in nonfictitious terms? This brings us to the other point of view expressed by Ihering when he speaks of the difficulty of "altering the concept," and particularly when, in the latter part of his discussion, he refers to the fiction as the "first step toward the mastery of a new thought."

Intellectual conservatism. A judge may adopt a fiction, not simply to avoid discommoding current notions, or for the

---

[24] There is some question whether the statute actually contained this fiction. Some take the view it was a later invention. See Buckland, *A Text-Book of Roman Law* (1921), p. 288.

purpose of concealing from himself or others the fact that he is legislating, but merely because he does not know how else to state and explain the new principle he is applying.

Perhaps I may be permitted at this juncture a somewhat unprepossessing simile. An elderly woman, not accustomed to attending social functions, is invited to a ball. The question arises as to what she shall wear. She finds that the only evening gown she owns is three years old and therefore somewhat out of style. Shall she buy a new, more modish gown or wear the old one? Let us assume that she decides to wear the old one, and conjecture what the motives back of her decision may be. First of all, we may suppose that she is the wife of a man in public life who wishes to achieve the air of substantiality that goes with a style of dress slightly out of date. If this were her motive in choosing the old dress, she would be actuated by considerations of *policy*. Second, it is possible that she feels herself somewhat out of sympathy with the innovations of a younger generation, and may associate what she regards as the laxer manners of a new day with the current fashions. By wearing her old dress she feels herself secure against the contaminations of a looser generation. In that case she would be actuated by an *emotional conservatism*. Again, she may decide to wear her old dress for the very simple reason that she dreads the inconvenience and expense of having a new dress made and fitted. Her motive in that case would be one of *convenience*. But last, she may be unacquainted with the new fashions, or may find their variety perplexing, and may, therefore, wear her old dress simply because she does not know what else to wear. In that event her conservatism would proceed from *intellectual* considerations.

Without intending any disrespect by so flippant a comparison, it seems to me that the same thing may be true of a judge. A judge may find himself forced to employ a fiction because of his inability to state his result in nonfictitious terms.

After all, the human mind is a machine subject to certain limitations. Perhaps the greatest of these limitations consists in the fact that human reason must always proceed by assimilating that which is unfamiliar to that which is already known. The situations that may be presented to a judge for decision are infinite in number; the intellectual equipment of rules, distinctions, concepts, and words, upon which the judge must rely in dealing with these situations, is limited and finite. We are forced to deal with new problems in terms of an existing conceptual apparatus which in the nature of things can never be entirely adequate for the future. "In order to understand, a certain degree of intellectual stability is needful, and stability cannot be obtained except at the sacrifice of truth. Truth is in a state of perpetual oscillation; its mobility, its variety is disconcerting. We cannot grasp it without falsifying it."[25] By "falsifying" reality I take it Tourtoulon means no more than that we find ourselves compelled to force new situations, which bob up out of the eternal flux of reality, into the confining framework of an existing intellectual apparatus.

It has already been shown how legal categories are constantly being remade to fit new conditions. Words like "possession," "estate," and "delivery" have, in the course of legal history, undergone rather obvious expansion. In a less obvious way this is true of all legal categories, and is going on constantly. Generally we do not use the term "fiction" in describing this process, for the simple reason that we are unaware of the process itself. This adaptation is so inconspicuous and gradual that it does not impress itself on our minds at all. It is only when a particular step in this process of adaptation is unusually bold and cutting that we cry "Fiction!" Often the term "fiction" involves, not simply the consciousness that a particular adaptation has taken place, but

[25] Tourtoulon, *Philosophy in the Development of Law* (1922), p. 395.

that it has taken place in an ungraceful and inelegant manner; that whereas *Category A* was rather roughly and violently stretched to cover the new situation, *Category B* would have covered it much more neatly—and with only a very little stretching. But the essential fact remains: the fiction is often but a cruder outcropping of a process of intellectual adaptation which goes on constantly without attracting attention.

The last statement may arouse opposition. Let us test it by considering as a concrete example what is probably the boldest fiction to be found in modern law—the "attractive nuisance doctrine."[26]

A young girl, living in an industrial district, is injured while playing with other children on a turntable maintained by a railway on an unfenced lot. A suit is brought on her behalf against the railway. Is the railway legally responsible for the injury? Let us attempt to follow the mental processes of the judge deciding this case.

The existing rules on the liability of a landowner for the condition of his premises are: The landowner owes a duty of care toward "invitees," toward those whom he has permitted, expressly or impliedly, to come on his land.[27] He owes no duty toward trespassers. It is clear that this child was legally a "trespasser," and therefore on the basis of these principles the railway would seem not to be liable. And yet, for some reason or other, the judge feels that the case is more like that of the "invitee" than that of the ordinary trespasser. Should

[26] This doctrine is discussed in Bohlen, "The Duty of a Landowner toward Those Entering His Premises of Their Own Right," 69 *Pa. L. Rev.* (1921), 340, 347; and J. Smith, "Liability of Landowners to Children Entering without Permission," 11 *Harv. L. Rev.* (1898), 349, 434. The discussion of this doctrine in the text should not be construed as an attempt to state what the proper rule is, or as a justification for the fiction often employed. It is a speculation concerning the possible mental processes of a hypothetical judge.

[27] The matter is not quite so simple as this, but we shall avoid complications that have no direct bearing on the problem discussed.

he then base his opinion on that ground? That would hardly do, because after all the child *was* a trespasser—there seems no escape from that. Shall the judge then say that the rule is different for children? That would be establishing a rather broad proposition. Who would be "children" within the meaning of the suggested rule? And would the landowner be responsible in a case where the child was aware of the danger?[28] Perhaps another tack would be better. Can we say that the distinguishing feature is the fact that the child was *attracted* to the land by the structure that resulted in her injury?[29] But again, where is the line to be drawn? People generally, and children in particular, may be "attracted" by any number of things. Perhaps at this point the judge's fancy wanders and the suggestion half-forms itself in his mind that we should make the test, in conventional legal language, whether the plaintiff was "reasonably" attracted, whether "as a child of reasonable and ordinary prudence . . ."—but this line of thought is dismissed as absurd.[30] Should we strike out boldly and say that the landowner owes a duty of care toward all trespassers when he knows, or ought to know, of the likelihood of their presence on his land? That, too, seems a rather broad doctrine. In a sense every landowner who has not securely fenced his property knows that trespassers may be on his land. Should the judge simply say, "For reasons that are essentially inarticulate and not wholly understood even

[28] "There is a tendency . . . to deny recovery where it is obvious that the injured child appreciated the danger and meddled with it in a spirit of bravado." Bohlen, *ibid.*, at p. 350.

[29] This is, of course, the notion embodied in the term "attractive nuisance," but it is by no means clear that this is the determinative factor in the decisions.

[30] Some of the distinctions actually developed by the courts seem only slightly less fanciful than the notion that our judge rejects. The decision in *City of Pekin* v. *McMahon* (1895) 154 Ill. 141, 150, seems to restrict liability to cases involving a device that, "when in motion," is "attractive to children by reason of their love of motion 'by other means than their own locomotion.'"

by myself, I decide for the plaintiff"? This is obviously asking a great deal.

Is it not possible that the judge in this dilemma may go back to the point from which he started, namely, the feeling that, in some way or other, this case is more like the case of an invitee than that of the ordinary trespasser? Why not say that the defendant must be "deemed to have invited" the child onto the land? This brings the case within the cover of existing doctrine and puts an end to these troublesome attempts to state a new principle.

This case has not been selected as typical of the process now under discussion, but rather because it is *not* typical. It is intended merely to show this: Even in the case of the crudest and most obvious fictions it is possible that the fiction may proceed from purely intellectual considerations. The judge, whose mental operations have been outlined, was not thinking of fooling others, nor was he carried away by an emotional desire to preserve existing doctrine. Neither was he considering the "convenience" of preserving current notions. Indeed, he may have been acutely aware that his own fiction would introduce inconvenience and obscurity into the law. He was simply seeking a solution for the case which was intellectually satisfying to himself. And that solution turned out to involve a forcing of the case into existing categories, instead of the creation of a new doctrine.

Developing fields of the law, fields where new social and business practices are necessitating a reconstruction of legal doctrine, nearly always present "artificial constructions," and, in many cases, outright fictions.[31] The doctrine of vicarious

[31] It is interesting to note that the same thing is true in the physical sciences. In physics gravitation has sometimes been described in the most metaphoric and, one is tempted to say, poetic terms. Gravitation "might be called a warp in space" (article "Ether" in the *Encyclopaedia Britannica*, 14th ed.); "Gravitation simply represents a continual effort of the universe to straighten itself out" (Dampier-Whetham, *A History*

liability for tort began with such notions as that the master should be "deemed negligent" for hiring a careless servant.[32] Fictions of this variety, constructions "feeling the way" toward some principle, may with justice be called *exploratory fictions*." Demogue likens such fictions to the empirical formulas of practical trades. "It frequently happens that we

---

of Science [1930], p. 427); "Gravitation, as explained by the general theory of relativity, is reduced to 'crinkles' in space-time" (Russell, *Philosophy* [1927], p. 278). We find the path of the earth around the sun, previously explained as due to a "tug" or "pull" of the sun, described as an effort of the earth to take the shortest route which the nature of surrounding space will permit. (Eddington, *The Nature of the Physical World* [1929], p. 148.)

Some will be inclined to say, "But these metaphors are merely expository. They are intended to make concrete for the reader who does not understand higher mathematics what could be more adequately and unmetaphorically expressed in a mathematical formula." But we have it from a mathematician of note that "Physics is mathematical, not because we know so much about the physical world, but because we know so little: it is only its mathematical properties that we can discover." Russell, *ibid.*, p. 157.

[32] The action of case will lie against a master, "in effect, for employing a careless servant." *Sharrod* v. *London etc. Ry. Co.* (1849) 4 Exch. 580, 585. Another fictitious construction which was employed in developing the doctrine of vicarious liability for tort was that the master "impliedly commands" whatever the servant does on his behalf. Wigmore, "Responsibility for Tortious Acts," 7 *Harv. L. Rev.* (1894), 315, 383.

It is interesting to note a similar development in Austrian law. "Section 1315 of the Austrian Civil Code limits the liability of employers for injuries caused by employees ... to negligence in selecting their employees." (Wurzel, "Juridical Thinking," in *The Science of Legal Method* [1917], pp. 286, 409.) Wurzel then points out how this section was gradually expanded, in part by such arguments as that "the very circumstances of an employee being negligent, proves that the employer was not careful in selecting him," until, in the case of corporations, we reach this culminating doctrine: "A juridical person can act only by agents, therefore it is impossible to distinguish between the acts of a corporation and those of its employees; consequently the corporation must be liable for all acts of its agents, the act of the agent is the act of the corporation." But the development did not stop even there. On the basis of this section the Austrian courts finally succeeded in imposing an absolute liability on street railways, on the ground that the mere operation of a street railway amounts to negligence! (*Ibid.*, p. 411.)

find the practical instrument for solving difficulties presented, before we discover the theoretic principles for explaining the excellence of these instruments. . . . The formula may be discovered before its *raison d'être*, as industrial processes may be known before their scientific explanation."[33]

A Peculiar Advantage of the Fiction

At this point it might be well to point out a peculiar virtue possessed by the fiction. The fiction is often likened to a scaffolding. This is usually with the implication that the fiction should be discarded as soon as possible, as when Gray says, "Such fictions are scaffolding—useful, almost necessary, in construction—but, after the building is erected, serving only to obscure it."[34] But the figure is apt in another sense. The fiction is like a scaffolding in that it can be removed with ease. The fiction seldom becomes a "vested interest"; it does not gather about it a group of partisan defenders. No one will mourn its passing. On the other hand, a construction that appears to be nonfictitious, even though from a scientific standpoint it may be as inadequate as the most daring fiction, is harder to displace.

> Certain writers have labored under the strange delusion that the law can be constructed upon objective realities . . . However, we affirm . . . that, quite the contrary, juridical theory is all the more objective when it presents itself as fictitious, and all the more delusive when it claims to do without fictions.[35]

[33] *Les notions fondamentales du droit privé*, pp. 242, 246.
[34] Gray, *Nature and Sources of the Law* (2d ed., 1921), p. 35.
[35] Tourtoulon, p. 295. Cf. "The artificiality of legal concepts is not an objection to their employment. Indeed, there is an advantage in purely artificial symbols. They carry with them only the amount of meaning contained in their definition, without the intellectual and emotional penumbra that more familiar terms always drag with them. The most dangerous concepts of the law are those like direct tax, republican form of government, interstate commerce, restraint of trade, and the

These are rather strong words, but they are probably justified. A doctrine that is plainly fictitious must seek its justification in considerations of social and economic policy; a doctrine that is nonfictitious often has a spurious self-evidence about it. And the fiction is always ready to give way to a more "adequate" explanation. The courts that have decided the "attractive nuisance" cases on the basis of a pretense may not have discovered the correct principle, but at least they have not obstructed its later discovery.

The Historical Legal Fiction Compared with Scientific Fictions

The function of the fiction, as effecting an adjustment between new situations and an existing conceptual structure, has a parallel in the methods of the natural scientist. The physicist finds it convenient, for certain purposes, to treat light and electricity as "vibrations." But vibrations of what? The only thing we can conceive of as vibrating is some kind of matter. And yet light and electricity pass through apparently empty space. Faced with this dilemma, the scientist adopted an expedient familiar enough to lawyers—he changed the facts to fit his theory.[36] He pretended that space was a kind of matter. But unlike the lawyer, the scientist has the habit of covering his pretenses with unfamiliar names. He called space "ether."[37]

---

like. They seem to be definite in themselves, but when we come to apply them, they prove most illusive." Cohen, "The Place of Logic in the Law," 29 *Harv. L. Rev.* (1916), 622, 634.

[36] There is no qualitative difference between the process called "changing the theory to fit the facts" and the process called "changing the facts to fit the theory." They are two ways of looking at the same procedure. But this scruple does not mar the utility of the expression as it is used in the text.

[37] "The regions in which there are no electrons and protons may be called 'ether' or 'empty space' as you prefer: the difference is only verbal." Russell, *Philosophy*, p. 107. But Eddington, like a conservative lawyer, has more respect for the fiction. "In any case the physicist

We shall return later to a more extended discussion of the "scientific fiction." But this illustration ought to be sufficient to indicate that we are in contact with a mental habit by no means confined to legal science. The motive of the scientific fiction is the same as that of the historical legal fiction proceeding from intellectual considerations; i.e., a new situation is made "thinkable" by converting it into familiar terms.

Other Devices Serving to Obscure the Growth of the Law

A writer in the *Harvard Law Review* once gave to the legal fiction a definition of surprising breadth. He called the fiction

---

does not conceive of space as void. Where it is empty of all else there is still the ether. Those who for some reason dislike the word ether, scatter mathematical symbols freely through the vacuum, and I presume that they must conceive some kind of characteristic background for these symbols" (p. 137).

It would be possible to make an interesting comparative historical study of the two fictions of corporate personality and the ether. For many centuries both notions were encumbered with all kinds of metaphysical and even supernatural connotations. As late as the time of Newton, "the idea of ether was still confused with Galen's concept of ethereal or psychic spirits." (Dampier-Whetham, p. 161. For Middle Age conceptions of corporate personality, see Dewey, "Corporate Legal Personality," p. 655.) In more recent times the realization has grown that neither idea "explains" anything at all, and that both fictions must be interpreted as terms of description merely. Karl Pearson calls the ether an "intellectual concept solely useful for the purpose of describing our perceptual routine." (*The Grammar of Science* [3d ed., 1911], Preface, p. v.) A modern German legal writer says there is no more "mystery" in the notion of corporate personality than there is in the sentence "The wagon carries a heavy load." In this sentence the word "wagon" is a unitary concept, linking together a conglomeration of wheels, bolts, boards, screws, and other parts, whereas the verb "carries" involves a metaphorical personification of the wagon. (Krückmann, *Institutionen des Bürgerlichen Gesetzbuches* [5th ed., 1929], pp. 81 *et seq.*) When this change in point of view has taken place our fictions have "died." And when they are dead, the question "Does the scientist really believe that space is filled with ether?" becomes as meaningless as the question "Does the lawyer really believe that a corporation is a person?" The scientist believes that space itself has properties, and he groups these properties about the word "ether"; the lawyer be-

"a device for attaining desired legal consequences or avoiding undesired legal consequences."[38] While this definition is so broad as to destroy the utility and significance of the term "fiction" altogether, it nevertheless recognizes an important truth, namely, that the fiction is but one of a large class of devices, all of which may serve, intentionally or otherwise, to obscure the growth of the law, and that it may often be a matter of accident whether a given reform takes place under the cover of the one device or the other.

First of all, the close affinity existing between the *fiction,* the *presumption,* and the doctrine of *estoppel* should be pointed out. Nearly any given reform in the law may be described as a redefinition of the "operative facts" upon which some legal consequence is predicated. For example, we may suppose that under existing law *Legal Consequence X* arises from *Facts A* and *B.* *A* and *B* are the facts that give rise to *Legal Consequence X.* It may now be found desirable to attribute the same consequence (*X*) to *Facts A* and *C.* For example, where previously liability for misrepresentation existed only in the case of an untruthful statement (= *Fact A*), made with knowledge of its untruth (= *Fact B*), it is now felt desirable to impose liability where there is an untruthful statement (= *Fact A*), made negligently (= *Fact C*). How can this reform be accomplished and yet leave the *form* of existing rules untouched? How can we preserve the appearance that *A* and *B* remain the operative facts? There are at least three distinct ways of doing this: (1) When *Facts A* and *C* are present, permit an allegation that *B* is present even though it is known that *B* is actually absent from the case. This is the method of the ordinary *fiction.* (2) Say that

---

lieves that the corporation must be treated in some respects like a "natural person," and he hangs this notion on the phrase "corporate personality."

[38] Mitchell, "The Fictions of the Law," 7 *Harv. L. Rev.* (1893), 249, 253.

Facts A and *C* raise a *presumption* that *B* is present.[39] (3)
State that the existence of *Facts A* and *C* "*estops*" the party
to deny that *Fact B* is present.[40] Any of these methods could
be employed in a given case. Any one of them would serve to
obscure the reform that has taken place, because each device
serves to preserve in form the notion that *Facts A* and *B*

[39] Numerous cases where the growth of the law has been obscured by
the use of presumptions are collected in Thayer, *Preliminary Treatise
on Evidence at the Common Law* (1898), pp. 313–52. In this development the presumption often starts as a rebuttable presumption; then,
through a gradual process of limiting rebuttal, it ends as a conclusive
presumption.

It is interesting to note that the device of the presumption has been
employed in accomplishing the particular reform used as an illustration
in the text, i.e., in creating a liability for honest misrepresentation. In
cases where a defendant has made a misrepresentation of fact and there
is no proof that he knew his statement was false (and, indeed, where
the evidence tends to show that he actually believed it), it has been
said that he must be "deemed to know" that his statement was false.
Bohlen, "Misrepresentation as Deceit, Negligence, or Warranty," *42
Harv. L. Rev.* (1929), 733, 744.

[40] The doctrine of "estoppel by deed" is an example of a case where
the growth of the law has been obscured through the use of the notion
of estoppel. We start with this sort of case: X purports to convey Blackacre to A, using a warranty deed. A goes into possession. In fact X had
no title at the time of the conveyance, but procures title later through
a conveyance from Y. X attempts to oust A, alleging that A has no title
because he, X, had none when he purported to convey to A. It was held
in this situation that X could not oust A, not because A had title, since
it was assumed that a conveyance could not operate to pass an after-
acquired title (the title from Y), but on the ground that although X
had title, he was "estopped" by his deed to A from asserting it against A.
(Coke Litt. 265a.) As a practical matter this had the same effect as a
holding that the later-acquired title had passed to A, but it preserved
the notion that a deed can affect only a title held at the time of the
conveyance. Later, however, the case arose where, before A had gone
into occupancy of the land, a stranger to title intruded himself in possession. Y having conveyed to X in the interim, A sues the intruder in
ejectment. On the basis of the previous cases it would seem, since A
had no title, and since the intruder could not be affected by the
"estoppel," A would lose the suit. It was held, however, for A, on the
ground that when X secured title from Y, this title "fed the estoppel"
and passed to A. (*Doe* v. *Oliver* [1829] 10 B. & C. 181. The conveyance
by X to A here had been by fine.) The net effect of this holding was
to recognize the very notion that the doctrine of estoppel by deed had

remain the foundations of the liability in question. Which device will be employed depends upon which is most expedient. Where *Facts A* and *C* can be said to have any tendency at all to prove *Fact B*, probably a presumption will be used,[41] although the presumption may involve the disadvantage that, if one is to preserve the notion that it is merely a "presumption," rebuttal, to some extent at least, will have to be permitted. If there is any conduct of the party which can form the basis for denying to him the privilege of disproving *B*, estoppel may be used.[42] If all else fails, there is left only the bald pretense of the fiction.

---

been developed to avoid—that a deed may pass an after-acquired title. But in order not to reveal how superfluous the notion of estoppel had become after this holding, the court said, not simply that title "passed," but that it passed by "feeding the estoppel." This is, in brief, the history of the doctrine of "feeding the estoppel," one of the most extravagant conceits to be found in the whole history of the law.

It should be pointed out that the estoppel was given a so-called "real" effect in England only in certain restricted cases, not including the ordinary bargain and sale deed; whereas in some of the American states the "real" effect is attributed to the ordinary warranty deed. Tiffany, *The Law of Real Property* (2d ed., 1920), II, sec. 545.

[41] But the tendency of *Facts A* and *C* to prove *B* may be quite remote. The "presumption of the lost grant" illustrates this point. Suppose that for twenty years A has used a roadway across B's land. The courts held in this situation that the twenty years' use by A, without interruption from B, raised a presumption that B had previously given A a written grant of the right, but that A was unable to produce this grant because it had been lost. (Blackstone, *Commentaries*, II, *265.)

[42] An appreciation of the close kinship of the presumption and the notion of estoppel is revealed in the following passage: "In some cases of conclusive legal presumption, a party is said to be *estopped*, and to have created an *estoppel* against himself. An estoppel is when a man has done some act which affords a conclusive presumption against himself in respect of the matter at issue. Thus, if a plaintiff disputes the title of the defendant to certain lands, and it appears that he holds them as tenant to the defendant, this affords a conclusive presumption, which he may not dispute, that his landlord is rightfully entitled; in other words, a tenant is estopped from disputing his landlord's title." (Thayer, p. 540.) In this same case we might treat the thing as a fiction by saying that the tenant must conduct himself *as if* the landlord had title, although it is known that he has not. Or again, we might eliminate all these methods of indirection and simply say: " 'Title' is only a way of

Another device that conceals the growth of the law is what Ihering calls the "feigned legal transaction."[43] A legal transaction originally created for one purpose is converted to a new use, first in isolated cases, and then, through a process of imitation, institutionally.[44] Thus, in Roman law the ceremony of the copper and scales was extended to a great number of uses only remotely connected with its original purpose. In English law we observe the growth of new forms of action out of old writs, and find such ingenious deflections of familiar devices to new purposes as the lease and release. In modern law the trust is constantly receiving new applications, and common instruments like the warehouse receipt[45] and the lease[46] are taking on new functions.

This diversion of existing devices to new uses differs from the ordinary fiction in that the reform arises out of the practice of individuals, rather than in the pronouncements of courts. But the role of the courts is not entirely passive. As Vinogradoff has said, "It is important to keep in mind that none of these acts . . . could have had any positive results, if the judges or magistrates did not make up their minds to connive at them, and to protect the beneficiaries from the undesirable consequences of their formal acts."[47] The difference

---

describing certain legal consequences; it is a purely legal concept. Therefore, as between the landlord and tenant the landlord *has* title, and there is no need to 'presume' or 'deem' that he has it, or to 'estop' the tenant from denying that he has it."

[43] *Geist des römischen Rechts auf den vershiedenen Stufen seiner Entwicklung* (6th ed., 1923), II[2], 504–37; III[1], 281–301.

[44] Sometimes a transaction is diverted to a new purpose, becomes "institutionalized" in its new function, and is then again diverted to a still different purpose, and again becomes "institutionalized" in its new form. In this case we have a feigned legal transaction in the second degree. *Ibid.*, III[1], 283.

[45] See Britton, "Equitable Liens," 8 *North Carolina L. Rev.* (1930), 388, 395, notes 20, 21.

[46] For example, in the law of oil and gas. See Summers, *The Law of Oil and Gas* (1927) ch. 7, for a discussion of the difficulty of fitting essentially new transactions into the existing "alphabet of the law."

[47] *Outlines of Historical Jurisprudence* (1920), I, 367.

between the feigned legal transaction and the fiction becomes even less conspicuous when we remember that most fictions have originated on the initiative of pleaders; the party alleges in his pleading a fact he knows to be false in the hope that the court will be willing to participate in his pretense and dispense with proof of the allegation.

The likeness existing between the ordinary fiction and the feigned legal transaction becomes particularly close when the latter takes the form of a lawsuit, as in the *in jure cessio* of the Roman law or the common recovery and fine of the English law. And in these cases frequently a fiction, of the ordinary sort, is invoked for the purpose of purging the transaction of requirements necessary to its original purpose but superfluous in its changed form, as where lease, entry, and ouster are pretended in the action of ejectment.[48]

However similar the fiction and the feigned legal transaction may be in some aspects, there yet exists between the two an interesting contrast. A fiction starts as a pretense, and may, through a process of linguistic development, end as a "fact." On the other hand, the feigned legal transaction may start as a fact and end as a pretense. That is to say, the process of diversion to a new purpose is usually so gradual, and proceeds with such cautious steps, that the parties concerned

---

[48] "The fiction by which formalities that have not been observed in reality are considered to have been, is of all times and all places." Tourtoulon, p. 389. Sometimes a symbolic significance is attributed to these "residuary formalities," i.e., formalities which were necessary and appropriate to the original purpose of the transaction, but which have become empty ceremonies. Ihering thinks that this symbolic significance is often invented to explain the presence of these formalities, where the real explanation is to be found in the purposes of the transaction in its original form. "Such residuary formalities may have their existence prolonged through the fact that a later time, which has lost the recollection of their historical origin, artificially attributes to them a symbolic meaning which was wholly foreign to them originally, and I am convinced that a great number of formalities are regarded as symbolic which in fact are nothing but residuary." (Ihering, II², 512.)

may themselves be unaware that they are giving the transaction a new function. At first there exists only a consciousness
that the transaction is being used for a purpose slightly different from the usual one.[49] But gradually the diversion becomes bolder, and a consciousness develops that the device
is really being employed for a new purpose, and that a distinct species of legal transaction has arisen. When this has
happened, the employment of the form of the old transaction comes to be looked upon as a pretense; an awareness
arises that the transaction is, in those parts appropriate to its
original purpose but inappropriate in its changed form, a
mere formality. It finally becomes, not merely a slightly diverted transaction, but a *feigned* transaction. But the preser-
vation throughout of the external form of the old transaction
serves to conceal or obscure the reform that is taking place
internally.[50]

[49] At first the parties may employ the transaction for the purpose of
achieving some legal consequence incidental to the transaction, taking
the other, and undesired, legal consequences "into the bargain," as it
were. But later, as the practice becomes institutionalized, the parties
begin to think of the transaction in terms of its new purpose. They
begin to expect of the courts that they should attribute to the transaction only those consequences appropriate to its new purpose; they begin to feel that the taking of undesired legal consequences "into the
bargain" is unnecessary. If the courts share this feeling and "protect
the beneficiaries from the undesirable consequences of their formal
acts," then we have, whether it is realized or not, the legal recognition
of a new, distinct transaction; the "alphabet of the law" has been en-
larged by a new letter. (Ihering, III[1], 294.)

[50] The remarks in the text should not be construed as a disapproval
of this process of growth. Disapproving of this method of development
would be like disapproving the ebb and flow of the tides. Ihering expresses the utility of this mode of growth in the following language:
"The certainty and security of any kind of progress depend upon historical continuity, upon an intimate connection between the present
and the past. Above all else, external form is one of the threads or
points of contact through which this continuity is made possible, for
while the inner, actual, historical point of contact and departure disappears more and more from the consciousness of the majority and
remains known only to a small group of scholars, *external form,* on
the other hand—as something visible and repeatedly occurring—

Another thing that obscures the process of lawmaking by a court is the frequently recurring notion that a court, in a particular case, is only determining the facts, not declaring law. Courts on the Continent, consciously or otherwise, have made the most extended use of this expedient.[51] Our own legal theory, that appellate courts determine only questions of law, has prevented the application of this notion in common-law cases. But in equity cases, where the facts are "opened up" on the appeal, our courts frequently claim to determine only the "facts" in cases where it is clear to an outsider that their determinations will be used in later cases as precedents, and therefore are "law."

One further point deserves mention before we conclude our discussion of devices, other than the fiction, which obscure the growth of the law. Every teacher of law knows how difficult it is to make students "stick to the facts" in answering examination questions, and how common the tendency is to eliminate difficult legal questions by the simple process of disregarding embarrassing facts. That the same thing is true to some extent of courts would require no detailed demonstration. Sporadic instances of this practice do not interest us here. But when this process of fact distortion becomes "institutional," when it is so often repeated as to furnish a substantial basis for predicting court action, then it becomes a matter of concern for the student of legal phenomena. In the note are appended several situations in which it is possible that we have an institutional tendency to fact distortion.[52] The

---

serves to preserve the consciousness of continuity in the minds of the people." (Ihering, II², 515.)

[51] Wurzel, pp. 286, 304, 335. And for a discussion of how the process of lawmaking is concealed in Germany under the doctrine of "stillschweigende Vereinbarung" or "Willenserklärung," see Weigelin, "Ueber rechtliche und sittliche Fiktionen," 18 Archiv für Rechts- und Wirtschaftsphilosophie (1924–25), 23.

[52] (I) It is supposed to be an elementary principle of law that death revokes an agency. If X hands a deed of land to T with instructions to

process differs from the ordinary fiction because the facts, as stated by the court, are regarded as the real facts of the case; the fiction, on the other hand, is an open and avowed pretense.

---

hand the deed to the grantee, A, on his, X's, death, this transaction cannot be legally effective after the death of X if X merely intended to make T his agent to deliver the deed. To create an effective arrangement X must intend a final "delivery" when he hands the deed to T; he must intend at that time to vest an estate in A. (Tiffany, II, sec. 462.) And yet those familiar with the cases in this field know that, when the case comes up *after the death of X,* the courts generally obligingly find that X reserved "no power of control" over the deed and intended a technical "delivery" when he handed it to T. On the other hand, when X, in his lifetime, attempts to recall the deed, the courts generally find that X merely made T his agent to hold the deed as depositary and that he may recall the deed.

As an illustration of this process, see *Thrush* v. *Thrush* (1912) 63 Oregon 143, 125 Pac. 267, 126 Pac. 994. In this case X attempted to recall the deed in his lifetime. A "tough-minded" judge on the first hearing held against X, and showed, by a careful review of the evidence, that X "reserved no power of control over the deed." On a rehearing the court, in a *per curiam* opinion, decided "upon a careful re-examination of the case" that X had reserved the power to revoke the arrangement, though the second opinion contains no reference to the facts of the case at all. But occasionally the whole court is toughminded. See *Stone* v. *Duvall* (1875) 77 Ill. 475.

(II) Where one occupies a portion of the land of another under a mistake as to his own boundaries, the general view is that he will gain title through the running of the statute of limitations only if he intended throughout to hold the land "whether he owned it or not." This rule seems to demand an inquiry of fact which is impossible. Who can say whether the possessor would have intended to keep the land if he had known that he did not own it, when as a matter of fact he thought throughout that he *did* own it? Yet the courts generally find in this situation that he intended to hold it whether he owned it or not. Sometimes a presumption to that effect is laid down; generally this purports to be a finding of fact without the aid of a presumption. See Tiffany, II, sec. 505, and Fuller, "Adverse Possession," 7 *Oregon L. Rev.* (1928), 329, 337, n. 36.

(III) Our courts do not openly avow the principle of Roman and Continental law that ingratitude by a donee gives the donor the power to revoke a gift. And yet, if we look to what our courts do, rather than what they say, it is arguable that the principle receives considerable recognition in this country. Frequently where the donee proves himself ungrateful, our courts are able to find that the gift was made on the condition of a certain line of conduct by the donee, or was induced by fraud.

Nonhistorical Fictions—Abbreviatory Fictions

Not all fictions have served to introduce reforms into the law; many of them have been invented for the purpose of expounding legal doctrine already in existence. And, on the other hand, many that once served a historical purpose have been retained for their descriptive power.

These descriptive fictions are often likened to a "convenient shorthand," and have been called "the algebra of the law."[53] The term "abbreviatory fictions" has been employed here with two distinct implications: first, as indicating that the purpose of the fiction is to avoid an inconvenient circumlocution, and second, as indicating that it is possible to avoid the fiction by "spelling the thing out," that the symbol *can* be expanded. Justice Holmes showed a keen appreciation of the function of the abbreviatory fiction when he said:

> A ship is not a person. It cannot do a wrong or make a contract. To say that a ship has committed a tort is merely a shorthand way of saying that you have decided to deal with it as if it had committed one, because some man has committed one in fact ... The contrary view would indicate that you really believed the fiction that a vessel had an independent personality as a fact behind the law.[54]

The German Civil Code contains a great number of such fictions.[55] To avoid an inconvenient periphrasis it is frequently provided that for certain purposes *Situation A* shall be treated as if it were *Situation B*. This dispenses with the need for a lengthy repetition of the legal consequences of *Situation B*. In Anglo-American law the number of fictions

[53] Tourtoulon, p. 385.
[54] *Tyler* v. *Judges of the Court of Registration* (1900) 175 Mass. 71, 77. Cf. the dissenting opinion of Loring, p. 82.
[55] These German statutory fictions are discussed in Bernhöft, *Zur Lehre von den Fiktionen* (1907), and Krückmann, "Wahrheit und Unwahrheit im Recht," 1 *Annalen der Philosophie* (1919), 114.

that are purely expository is probably rather small. "Corporate personality" (as it is understood today), "constructive notice," and many of the doctrines of the "relation back" of title may fairly be called abbreviatory devices. Perhaps other fictions could be enumerated here. But since so many of our fictions, even when they serve an expository purpose, remain tinged with a persuasive element, or continue to be colored by their historical functions, an adequate discussion would require treatment of each fiction separately and would lead us too far astray from our main purpose.

The utility of an abbreviatory fiction should be judged purely in terms of its capacity to effect a felicitous description, by the inquiry whether it strikes a convenient balance between an inaptly periphrastic accuracy and a misleading vividness. "If it is very good, it will outline concrete provisions of the law wonderfully well; if it is bad, it will outline them very clumsily, and it will be necessary to complement it with a great number of exceptions in order to give it its correct value."[56]

Ihering applied to the kind of linguistic device now under discussion the term "dogmatic fiction." His example has not been followed here for two reasons. First, Ihering's own discussion tends to indicate that he may be including under the term "dogmatic fiction" two notions that have been separated here, i.e., the fiction produced historically by "intellectual conservatism" (the fiction that makes a new legal conclusion "thinkable" by converting it into familiar terms), and the abbreviatory fiction.[57] While it must be admitted that the two functions of the fiction are closely related,[58] it seems con-

---

[56] Tourtoulon, p. 391.

[57] Ihering, III[1], 308. The only definition of the purpose of the "dogmatic fiction" given by him is: "der Zweck der Fiktion ist hier nicht Erleichterung der Anknüpfung eines neuen Rechtssatzes an das bisherige Recht, sondern *Erleichterung der juristischen Vorstellung*" (italics mine).

[58] The relation between the two may be made clearer by saying that the abbreviatory fiction is produced by considerations of convenience

venient to separate off under the heading of "abbreviatory fictions" those cases where the fiction may be avoided if one is willing to pay the price of a more lengthy and awkward description. Second, the term "dogmatic" seems to imply that the fiction has some force or power beyond that of mere description. Gray thought that "dogmatic fictions, instead of being obstacles to symmetrical classification, have been introduced and used *as aids to it*."[59] With this it is difficult to agree. Any fiction, by virtue of the fact that it *is* a fiction, i.e., an inadequate description of the relations involved, is an obstacle to scientific classification. The fiction has no mystic power to promote good classification. The class formed by the corporation and the natural person may be described without using the word "person," and the use of the word "person," insofar as it tends to imply a complete equality between the corporation and the "natural person," is "an obstacle to symmetrical classification." The function of the abbreviatory fiction is to make concrete and vivid a classification that might be described more adequately in terms that would not be felt as fictitious.

Apologetic or Merciful Fictions

Are all nonhistorical fictions merely expository? That seems to have been the assumption of Ihering. Yet there are some fictions which cannot be identified as ever having introduced

---

in *expression,* while the historical fiction proceeding from intellectual conservatism is produced by considerations of convenience in *conception.*

This suggests the question: Are there fictions which facilitate conception, and not merely expression, but which are nonhistorical, which cannot be said to have introduced any definite change in the law? I know of but one, namely, the notion that in interpreting legislation a court must treat a statute *as if it were* a message from someone, whether that "someone" be called "the sovereign," "the state," "the Volksgeist," or, more prosaically, simply "the legislator." A message from no one is an idea so foreign to ordinary conceptions that we refuse to embrace it. See Kornfeld, *Allgemeine Rechtslehre und Jurisprudenz* (1920), p. 8.

[59] *Nature and Sources of the Law* (2d ed., 1921), p. 35.

a reform into the law, and which, at the same time, are not merely expository or descriptive. For example, what reform was accomplished by the fiction that "everyone is presumed to know the law"? And is it a clearer exposition of the thought involved than to say that ignorance of the law is juristically immaterial?

A fiction of this sort may be called an apologetic or merciful fiction. It apologizes for the necessity in which the law finds itself of attributing to the acts of parties legal consequences that they could not even remotely have anticipated. Although, as understood by the lawyer, this "presumption" merely means that ignorance of the law is immaterial, its formulation as a presumption of knowledge proceeds from the same tactful impulse that leads a generous creditor to say, "Let us consider the debt paid," instead of, "I release you from the debt." The administration of the law would be a much more pleasant task if the legal consequences attributed to the acts of parties were such as the parties might have foreseen. This fiction is a way of obscuring the unpleasant truth that this cannot be the case.

> It is an essentially human tendency to refuse to believe sad events and to invent happy ones. What the lawmaker sometimes tries to do is precisely this—to efface unfortunate realities as far as possible and to evoke the shades of fortunate realities which have not been achieved . . . While the fiction is a subtle instrument of juridical technique, it is also clearly the expression of a desire inherent in human nature, the desire to efface unpleasant realities and evoke imaginary good fortune.[60]

[60] Tourtoulon, p. 386. Tourtoulon seems, however, to carry this notion to extremes when he suggests that the *fictio legis Corneliae* had its origin in the disinclination of the Romans to admit the unpleasant fact that a Roman soldier *could* be captured.

Malinowski, in "The Problem of Meaning in Primitive Languages" (a supplement to Ogden and Richards, *The Meaning of Meaning* [2d ed., 1927], pp. 296, 314) suggests that one function of language is simply to *say something*, to overcome the disagreeable tension that accom-

The fiction that "the king can do no wrong" is probably of the same type. By creating in the mind a state of vacillation between the moral and legalistic ideas of "wrong," it secures for the latter a persuasive force legitimately coming to the former. It is a way of apologizing for the fact that the king enjoys a legal status different from that of his subjects.[61]

Other Motives for the Fiction—Fanciful and Habitual Fictions

Has our discussion exhausted the motives for the fiction? So far, we have assumed always that the motive is a serious one. But is this always the case? Hobbes regarded one of the "speciall uses of Speech" as "to please and delight ourselves, and others, by playing with our words, for pleasure or ornament, innocently."[62] Can it be that courts have occasionally resorted to fiction for the mere amusement afforded thereby? Tourtoulon suggests that at times the fiction may be "but a way the jurist has of amusing himself," but adds in a palliative vein that it is "something in itself to lighten the juridical burden."[63] Austin found that some fictions could only be explained as attributable to the "active and sportive fancies of their grave and venerable authors."[64] When Blackstone states that the king cannot be nonsuited for failing to appear in a case because he has the legal quality of ubiquity, and that "His majesty in the eye of the law is always present in all his

---

panies silence. "The modern English expression, 'Nice day today' or the Melanesian phrase, 'Whence comest thou?' is needed to get over the strange and unpleasant tension which men feel when facing each other in silence." Perhaps the presumption that everyone knows the law is attributable to a desire to *say something* in answer to the reproach that the law attributes consequences to the acts of individuals which the individuals concerned could not have foreseen.

[61] But the fiction had other uses; see Blackstone, I, *246.
[62] *Leviathan*, ch. IV.
[63] Tourtoulon, p. 385.
[64] *Lectures on Jurisprudence*, II, 611.

courts,"[65] we seem to detect a vein of unrestrained fancy not compatible with entire seriousness. And yet fictions attributable to a mere desire for amusement are probably very uncommon. The rather serious business of interfering in the lives of others, and the necessity of justifying that interference at every step, is enough to restrain whatever tendencies toward fantasy the average judge may have.

On the other hand, is it safe to assume that there is a motive *of some sort* behind every fiction? Have not many of our fictions become so common and so much a matter of habit that they are frequently repeated by the courts without any particular motive at all? For example, although originally the maxim, "Everyone is presumed to know the law," was but a perverted form of the doctrine that ignorance of the law is immaterial, the fictional method of stating the rule has become so habitual that we are not at all surprised to find a court reversing the thing and stating, "It is axiomatic . . . that 'every man is presumed to know the law' and of this 'ignorance of the law does not excuse' *is but a sequence.*"[66]

The statute of 13 Elizabeth 1, c. 5, made voidable certain "fraudulent conveyances," i.e., conveyances made with the intent to defeat the claims of creditors. The English courts, however, went considerably beyond the statute and held certain conveyances voidable at the option of creditors where there was in fact no fraudulent intent. The desirability of bringing these cases within the wording of the act, however, led the courts to speak of "constructive fraud," or a "fraud in contemplation of law."[67] This kind of talk became in time so common that the habit grew up of treating voidability wherever possible as founded on "fraud, actual or constructive."

---

[65] *Commentaries*, I, *270.
[66] Wolverton, J., in *Scott* v. *Ford* (1904) 45 Or. 531, 536, 78 Pac. 742, 744. Italics supplied.
[67] Bigelow, *Fraudulent Conveyances* (1911), sec. 6, p. 73.

Indeed, this linguistic habit became so strong that it was carried over into legislation, and we find recording statutes providing that an unrecorded deed should be "deemed fraudulent" as to subsequent bona fide purchasers.[68] Even a scientific piece of legislation like the Uniform Fraudulent Conveyances Act makes a conveyance without consideration by one who is insolvent "fraudulent," "without regard to his actual intent."[69] It would probably be a mistake to suppose that this language is due either to a desire to make the meaning of the statute clear (since surely the word "voidable" would be better in that respect than "fraudulent"), or to any impulse other than that of mere habit and imitation.

General and Special Fictions

Dean Pound has taken a useful distinction between general and special fictions.

> If we look narrowly at the fictions by means of which the law has grown in the past, we may divide them into general fictions—fictions under which a general course of procedure or general doctrines have grown up; and particular or special fictions—fictions which have enabled a new rule to grow up in particular cases.[70]

An example of a general fiction is the notion of an appeal to "higher law" which accompanied the reforms effected by

[68] Thus the statute of 7 Anne c. 20 (1708) provided that an unrecorded deed should be "adjudged fraudulent and void against any subsequent purchaser or mortgagee for valuable consideration." The more common language of the American recording statutes speaks merely in terms of voidability and says nothing of "fraud."

[69] Sec. 5. The drafters of the act speak of the "awkward method" which had been developed by the courts for dealing with cases of this sort. The courts had spoken of "presumptions of fraud," or of "fraud in contemplation of the law." Under the act all of this becomes obsolete; the act of the insolvent is "fraudulent without regard to his actual intent."

[70] "Spurious Interpretation," 7 Col. L. Rev. (1907), 379, 383; Interpretations of Legal History (1923), pp. 131–36.

courts of chancery in England and by the praetor in Rome, the notion that equity came not to destroy the law but to fulfill it.[71]

The general fiction of Anglo-American jurisprudence that courts do not "make" law but only "discover" or "declare" it has been the cause of innumerable special fictions designed to conceal the process of legislation that actually goes on in the courts. It is interesting to note that a similar general fiction on the Continent, that courts do not "make" law but only "interpret" a statutory system, has had precisely the opposite effect, i.e., it has dispensed with the necessity for special or particular fictions. The courts "do not utilize the device of the fiction to fill in a gap in the statute. When such a necessity is imposed on them they have recourse to a means which serves them in every situation: the argument from the text. ... The judges stop at no subtlety which will give the text the desired sense."[72]

The tendency of the legal mind to treat legal results wherever possible as dependent upon "the intent of the parties" may perhaps be called a general fiction. "This unexpressed intention which is not, for the greater part, present to the mind of the party himself at the moment of concluding the contract"[73] plays an important role in modern law. What

[71] Maitland, *Lectures on Equity* (1909), p. 18.

[72] Lecocq, *De la fiction comme procédé juridique* (1914), p. 251.

[73] Sohm, "Institutes of Roman Law" (Ledlie's transl.) sec. 15, quoted from Pound, "Law as Developed in Juristic Thought" 30 *Harv. L. Rev.* (1917), 201, 211, n. 34.
How unreal the inquiry into "intent" may at times become is admirably illustrated in the following passage from Wurzel: "A young girl in the lower walks of life becomes engaged to a clerk. In order to enable him to establish a home she turns over to him her savings, and together they establish themselves in some business. They have no success in this, and as a result the engagement is broken off. Now the girl sues her former fiancé for a return of the money and the answer is that it was lost in the partnership business.
"Now the judge will have to find whether the turning over of the money was intended as a loan; or whether it was meant to be the ad-

is the explanation for this persistent tendency to attribute legal dispositions to a nonexistent intent? What considerations are really actuating courts when they purport to investigate the "intent of the parties" and perhaps believe that they are doing no more? These questions have not received the attention in legal studies that they deserve.

Procedural Fictions

The ordinary procedural pretense serves to facilitate an alteration in "substantive law." By permitting an allegation of "invitation" in the "attractive nuisance" cases, the courts accomplished a change in the substantive rules concerning the liability of a landowner. But procedure does not lack its own fictions, serving, as it were, exclusively procedural ends. "Constructive service" is an example of such a fiction. And perhaps it may be said that procedure has been dominated by one "general" fiction; the notion—inherited from primitive law—that a trial is the submission of a controversy by the consent of the parties. While this notion is not openly avowed today and is patently inconsistent with modern practice, it is possible to argue that it still influences procedural modes of speech, and in a kind of residuary and attenuated form lives on out of the past.[74]

---

vancement of a marriage portion; or whether the business was to belong to the plaintiff with the defendant as partner; or whether the money was invested as a limited partnership fund, or whatever other possibilities may exist. The judge has to answer all these questions, although perhaps, nay in all probability, the intention of the parties at the time when the money was turned over was in no wise definitely fixed. What was in their minds was nothing more than that they loved each other, had perfect mutual confidence, were going to get married, and that it made no difference whatever in whose pocket the money was kept. In short, the thinking and willing of the two young people did not proceed according to the forms of the Roman Law." ("Juridical Thinking" in *The Science of Legal Method,* p. 399.)

[74] A discussion of the influence on modern German procedure of the notion involved in the Roman *litis contestatio* (as a pretended contract of submission) will be found in Bülow, "Civilprozessualische Fiktionen

Statutory Fictions

In the debates preceding the adoption of the French Civil Code the question was raised whether it was legitimate to employ fictions in legislation. Toullier protested, "The fiction is unworthy of the majesty of the legislator; he has no need to pretend, he commands." To which Marcadé responded, "It is precisely because the legislator is all-powerful that he may create as many fictions as he wishes."[75] In accordance with the notion that the legislator "commands" or is "all-powerful," it is often assumed that if fictions *are* found in legislation they are to be construed as expository devices—mere conveniences of expression. Somló likens the position of the legislator to a gentleman giving instructions to his servant. "If I have given my servant permission to take Sundays off I can later annex an exception expressly and openly, or I can clothe

---

und Wahrheiten," 62 *Archiv für die civilistische Praxis* (1879), 1, especially under the heading "Die Fiktion der Litiscontestation und der Einlassung," at p. 11.

In early law, owing to the influence of the idea mentioned above, the default judgment was unknown. "One thing our law would not do; the obvious thing. It would exhaust its terrors in the endeavor to make the defendant appear, but it would not give judgment against him until he had appeared, and, if he was obstinate enough to endure imprisonment or outlawry, he could deprive the plaintiff of his remedy." (Pollock and Maitland, *The History of English Law* [2d ed., 1898], II, 594.) We do the "obvious thing" now; we do not hesitate to enter a default judgment against the nonappearing defendant. But the old notion of "consent" lives on in our conceptions of "process." In 1923 a statute was passed in Massachusetts which provided that the operation of a motor vehicle by a nonresident within the state should "be deemed equivalent to an appointment . . . of the registrar" of the state as agent to receive service of process. See Scott, "Jurisdiction over Non-resident Motorists," 39 *Harv. L. Rev.* (1926), 563.

An analytical discussion of the fictions of modern German procedural law will be found in Baumhoer, "Die Fiktion im Straf- und Prozessrecht," Beiheft Nr. 24 to the *Archiv für Rechts- und Wirtschaftsphilosophie* (1930). Most of the "fictions" discussed in this pamphlet are fictions in the Vaihingerian sense only; they are what most people would call "abstractions" or "concepts."

[75] Lecocq, p. 246.

it in the form that this or that workday shall be regarded as a Sunday, or that this or that Sunday shall be deemed a workday."[76] This illustration he regards as revealing the true character of legislative fictions.

How realistic a picture does this give of the position of the legislator? One of the oldest and most audacious of the fictions of the Roman law was statutory, the fictio legis Corneliae. Was this fiction a mere convenience of expression?[77] The true explanation would seem to be that given by Demogue. "The legislator himself did not dare to touch the edifice of the ancient law."[78] This "all-powerful" right of the legislator to "command" is usually more apparent to others than to himself, and is often the figment of the historian of a later epoch who ignores the realities of the political life out of which the legislation arose.

In 1922 a statute regulating the leasing of dwellings was passed in Germany. This act provided that the decisions of the tribunal constituted to administer it should be deemed to form a part of every contract of leasing entered into after the passage of the statute. This provision avoided doing open violence to the fiction, so strenuously adhered to on the Continent, that courts do not make law.[79] English legal history is strewn with statutory reforms taking cumbersome and artificial forms to conceal the fact that an alteration of the law is taking place. An early English statute designed to correct

[76] *Juristische Grundlehre* (2d ed., 1927), p. 526.
[77] See the remarks under the heading "The Motive of Convenience," pp. 59–63.
[78] *Les notions fondamentales du droit privé* (1911), p. 239. As has been pointed out previously, there is some doubt whether the fiction was really a part of the statute. See Buckland, *A Text-Book of Roman Law*, p. 288. And cf. Tourtoulon's rather fanciful explanation of this fiction, *supra*, note 60.
[79] Hofacker, "Fiktionen im Recht," *4 Annalen der Philosophie* (1925), 475. The statute referred to is the Reichsmietengesetz vom 24 März 1922, sec. 15. Hofacker calls this "eine ganz wüste Fiktion."

the inconveniences of the principle—so common in undeveloped systems of law—that no judgment may be had
against a defendant who does not appear in court, provided
that where the defendant failed to appear after service of
process the plaintiff might appear for him![80] The Veterans
Bill, vetoed by President Hoover in June 1930, provided that
in the case of veterans of World War I afflicted with certain
diseases between 1925 and 1930 a conclusive presumption
should be raised that these diseases originated in service.[81]
These illustrations, taken from different epochs and from
widely separated regions, ought to dispel the notion that
statutory fictions are always merely expository.

[80] See the statutes 5 George II c. 27 and 12 George I c. 29. In this
connection mention should be made of the English statutes enlarging
the powers of courts of equity. 11 George IV & 1 Will. IV c. 36, and
11 George IV & 1 Will. IV c. 60. These statutes provided that where
a defendant had been ordered to execute a conveyance and had refused, or was unable to make, the conveyance, the court might appoint
a master to make the conveyance *for the defendant*. The simpler recourse would have provided that the court might decree title to be in
the plaintiff, without any act by or for the defendant. But the statute
preserved in form the notion that a court of equity has no power to
make a declaration of right, but acts only *in personam*, i.e., by coercing
the party into exercising his own legal powers. That this notion is not
confined to Anglo-American law is indicated in the following quotation
from a treatise on German procedure: "Where there is a decree ordering the exercise of a power (for example, directing the making of a
conveyance, or the giving or cancellation of a mortgage), no execution
or performance [of the decree] takes place, but through the legal force
of the decree the fiction that the power has been exercised [by the de-
fendant] is assumed." Seuffert, "Zivilprozessrecht," in *Die Kultur der
Gegenwart*, II[8]—*Systematische Rechtswissenschaft* (1906), 162, 188.

[81] In his message to Congress President Hoover stated that the presumption involved in the bill "constitutes a wholly false and fictitious
basis for legislation," and added, "The spectacle of the government
practicing subterfuge in order to say that what did not happen in the
war did happen in the war impairs the integrity of government, re-
duces the respect for government and undermines the morale of all the
people." *New York Times*, June 27, 1930, p. 6.

3. Is Fiction an Indispensable Instrument of Human Thinking?

Without in the least wanting to be a philosopher, either in fact or in name, the scientist is under a strong compulsion to examine critically the processes through which his knowledge is won and extended.[1]

In writing of the legal fiction it is easy to slip into the past tense. We have, without knowing exactly why, a feeling that the fiction belongs to a stage in the development of the law that is now safely passed.[2] We tend to assume that the primary interest of the subject is historical. Yet a moment's reflection is sufficient to show that there is little basis for this feeling. We know that the fiction is being used in contemporary law. Certainly we have no reason to expect the intervention of some miracle which will change the minds of judges and legal thinkers overnight. If judges and legal writers have used the fiction in the past, and are using it now, they will probably continue to use it in the future.

What, then, is the source of this impression that the fiction is a thing of the past? I suspect that the answer is twofold. In the first place, the fiction always seems pitiably obvious and naïve—in retrospect. It seems difficult to imagine that intelligent human beings could be "deceived by the whimsical device of the fiction"—when one is viewing the thing from the perspective of history. We easily forget that the fiction is by no means so transparent to the man who resorts

[1] Mach, *Erkenntnis und Irrtum* (2d ed., 1906), Vorwort, p. v.
[2] "They [legal fictions] are now recognized as the blundering devices of an unphilosophic age, which had not yet learned from science to value truth for its own sake." Phelps, *Juridical Equity* (1894), p. 206.

to it in his struggle to solve an embarrassing problem. To him the fiction often seems, not simply the easiest way out of his difficulties, but the only way out.

The other reason why we tend to relegate the fiction to the past lies in our failure to realize that the law will be faced, in the future, with essentially *new* situations. The fiction is generally the product of the law's struggles with *new* problems. Since we cannot foresee *what* changes are destined to take place in our social and economic structure, we tend to ignore in our calculations the probability, indeed, certainty, that changes of some sort will occur and that with them essentially new problems will be presented to the courts.

The age of the legal fiction is not over. We are not dealing with a topic of antiquarian interest merely. We are in contact with a fundamental trait of human reason. To understand the function of the legal fiction we must undertake an examination of the processes of human thought generally. Particularly will it be necessary to study the use of similar devices in other fields of science. In such a study there can be no better starting point than Vaihinger's philosophy of "As If."

Vaihinger's Philosophy of "As If"

Hans Vaihinger's book ("Die Philosophie des Als Ob")[3] was written in the period 1876–78 and was first published in

---

[3] The work is now in its eighth edition. References in this article are to the paging of the fourth edition of 1920. The book has not been altered since its original publication. Unfortunately, the English translation by C. K. Ogden, published in 1924, is quite unsatisfactory. For example, on page 3 of Ogden's translation we find that the phrase "mit dem objektiven Sein sich decken" has been translated as "clothed with objectivity"! This blunder occurs at a rather crucial point in Vaihinger's exposition, because Vaihinger is arguing that whereas our theories and ideas must "be congruent with objective reality," they need not, and indeed cannot, "mirror" reality.

A popular exposition of Vaihinger's philosophy will be found in ch. III of Havelock Ellis's *The Dance of Life* (Modern Library ed., 1929).

1911. It is a systematic study of the influence of the fiction in all the departments of human intellectual activity. The book made a pronounced impression in German philosophic circles, and had an especially strong influence on German legal thinking. Some idea of the importance of Vaihinger in modern German legal thought may be gained from the appended bibliography of works discussing the application of his philosophy to legal problems.[4] Vaihinger taught German

[4] The following books and articles are concerned primarily with the legal aspects of Vaihinger's philosophy: Baumhoer, "Die Fiktion im Straf- und Prozessrecht," Beiheft Nr. 24 to the *Archiv für Rechts- und Wirtschaftsphilosophie* (1930); Fischer, "Fiktionen und Bilder in der Rechtswissenschaft," 117 *Archiv für die zivilistische Praxis* (1919), 143; Hofacker, "Fiktionen im Recht," 4 *Annalen der Philosophie* (1925), 475; Kelsen, "Zur Theorie der Juristischen Fiktionen," 1 *Annalen der Philosophie* (1919), 630; Krückmann, "Das juristische Kausalproblem als Problem der passendsten Fiktion," 37 *Zeitschrift für die ges. Strafrechtswissenschaft* (1916), 353; Krückmann, "Einheit, Subjekt, Person," *Archiv für die zivilistische Praxis* (1916), 143; Krückmann, "Wahrheit und Unwahrheit im Recht," 1 *Annalen der Philosophie* (1919), 114; Krückmann, "Fiktionen und Bilder in der Rechtswissenschaft," 3 *Annalen der Philosophie* (1922), 418; Mallachow, "Zur Metajurisprudenz und Rechtsphilosophie," 1 *Annalen der Philosophie* (1919), 664; Mallachow, *Rechtserkenntnistheorie und Fiktionslehre* (1922); Mannheim, "Die Philosophie des Als-Ob und ihre Bedeutung für das Strafrecht," 11 *Aschaffenburgs Mon. Schr.* (1914), 1; Salomon, "Die Rechtswissenschaft und die Philosophie des Als-Ob," 13 *Archiv für Rechts- und Wirtschaftsphilosophie* (1919), 227; Sauer, "Rechtswissenschaft und Als-Ob-Philosophie," 41 *Zeitschrift für die ges. Strafrechtswissenschaft* (1920), 423; Strauch, *Die Philosophie des "Als Ob" und die haupsächlichsten Probleme der Rechtswissenschaft* (1923); Sturm, *Fiktion und Vergleich in der Rechtswissenschaft* (1915); Sturm, "Zur Weltanschauung des Als-Ob im Recht," 3 *Annalen der Philosophie* (1922), 148; Weigelin, "Ueber rechtliche und sittliche Fiktionen," 18 *Archiv für Rechts- und Wirtschaftsphilosophie* (1924-25), 23 (this article does not mention Vaihinger directly, but is based on secondary sources); Weyr, "Bemerkungen zu H. Vaihinger's Theorie der juristischen Fiktionen," 9 *Rhein. Z. für Ziv.- und Proz.- R.* (1917-18), 1. (The bibliography given above is not complete, but may be supplemented by the list of works given in Baumhoer, *supra.*)
    The following works contain incidental discussions of Vaihinger's philosophy at the places indicated: Kornfeld, *Allgemeine Rechtslehre und Jurisprudenz* (1920), pp. 45-60; Krückmann, *Institutionen des Bürgerlichen Gesetzbuches* (5th ed., 1929), pp. 43-44; Tourtoulon,

legal science how to use its own intellectual tools; he did
much to dispel the "unconscious metaphysics" which inheres
in undisciplined thinking. Where Ihering taught German
lawyers to think of legal rules in terms of purpose, Vaihinger
taught them to regard the conceptual structure of legal
thought itself as a means to an end.

The brief account of Vaihinger's philosophy that follows
reveals at once the similarity between his views and those
of American pragmatism. Indeed, it has been suggested that
he is more pragmatic than the American school because,
while American pragmatism has always insisted upon the
importance of details and the danger of generalities, on the
whole its proponents have confined themselves—so far as
the study of methodology is concerned—to observations
concerning the nature of thinking in general; Vaihinger, on
the other hand, undertakes a critical and painstaking examination of the processes of thought actually employed in the
various sciences.[5] He has obtained his generalizations about
human thinking, not by deduction from some premise concerning the nature of thought in general, but from an examination of the ways and byways of thought in particular
sciences. It is characteristic of him that he defended the view
that philosophy should not be taught as a separate subject,
but ought rather to form a supplemental study of methodology in connection with the particular branches of science.

I shall not attempt to limit myself strictly to Vaihinger's
work. I shall not hesitate to employ illustrations and quotations from other modern thinkers. My excuse for doing this is

---

Philosophy in the Development of Law (1922; a translation of *Les prin-
cipes philosophiques de l'histoire du droit,* 1919), pp. 644–53. See also
Professor Cohen's Introduction to this work, pp. xxx–xxxi.

[5] Jacoby, "Der amerikanische Pragmatismus und die Philosophie des
Als Ob," *147 Zeitschrift für Philosophie und philosophische Kritik*
(1912), 172.

simply that my primary purpose is to present, as forcibly as possible, a point of view. This supplementation of Vaihinger need not result in any distortion of his views.[6]

Vaihinger's Problem

The question which Vaihinger set out to answer was: How does it come about that with consciously false ideas we are yet able to reach conclusions that are "right," i.e., conclusions which seem to be in harmony with nature and which appeal to us as "truth"? Before we attempt to give Vaihinger's answer to this question it will be well to retrace the steps which led him to a formulation of the problem. As Vaihinger himself

---

[6] Perhaps it would be truer to the spirit of Vaihinger to say that the distortion will be no greater than is justified by our present purposes. It might be said at this point that Vaihinger's philosophy is not presented in this article with the notion that it constitutes a revolutionary point of view. Much that Vaihinger has to say, perhaps all of it, may be found in other modern thinkers. But Vaihinger's peculiar virtue consists in his power of exposition. Just as the psychologist can learn much about normal mental life by a study of abnormal conditions, so Vaihinger, starting with those aberrations of thought we call "fictions," was able to learn much about the more "normal" processes of thought. And—what is in point here—this mode of approach has peculiar pedagogical advantages. The reader is not merely told that thinking is "instrumental"; he is made to see it. The fiction is like a projecting stratum of rock which enables the geologist to know what is beneath the surface. In the fiction we find human thought struggling, as it were, "in the open," and by a study of the fiction we can gain an insight into the normal workings of thought which would otherwise be inaccessible to us.

Before taking up our exposition of Vaihinger it might also be well to add that Vaihinger's philosophy is not presented as a panacea for all the ills that beset legal thinking. Perhaps American legal scholars are a little tired of panaceas. But I am firmly convinced that a study of Vaihinger will make one a *better* legal thinker. In the following discussion no attempt is made to trace the relations of Vaihinger to other philosophers. This would be foreign to the purpose of the present article and beyond my capacities. Vaihinger's special indebtednesses are to Kant and Lange. If it can be said that Vaihinger has merely restored the "radical" Kant and has limbered up his categories through the introduction of the notion of evolution, his contribution would not, on that account, be the less worthy of attention.

says, the putting of the question is fully as important as its answer; a clear realization of the nature of a problem is often the most important step toward its solution.

We may suppose that Vaihinger's attention was first attracted to the more obvious kinds of fictions. In two apparently dissimilar fields, law and mathematics, we find the most extended use of fictions, or, if the expression is preferred, of hypotheses that are known to be false. The law has always been notorious as a field of fiction and pretense. Not only are the doctrines of positive law interwoven with fictions, but theories of the nature of law in general have always contained a plentiful admixture of fiction. Law is regarded as emanating from a mystic *Volksgeist*, or is the command of an intangible, undiscoverable sovereign. In mathematics we find exceedingly useful results deduced from apparently absurd notions, such as infinity, negative numbers, $\sqrt{-1}$, and the fourth dimension. The curve is rendered tractable to calculation by a tautological and apparently self-contradictory assumption that it is composed of a series of infinitely short straight lines.

When we turn to other sciences, we do not find the situation to be different. In theories of the state there appears the constantly recurring notion of the Social Compact, a notion which perhaps was never given full credence as a historical fact by anyone, but which has nevertheless had the most profound, and perhaps beneficial, influence on the history of human thought. Various economists have founded their systems upon a theory that man is an "economic animal," constantly seeking his own advantage—an assumption that is at least false insofar as it ignores the undoubted fact that man often acts from mere habit and custom, even if one were willing to concede the absence of altruism in human nature.

In the physical sciences, we find the mathematical fictions applied with great success, and new imaginative concepts, such as that of the ether, added. In the new physics the tendency toward an apparently unbridled imagination seems to have undergone a great development. Vaihinger regards both the fourth dimension and the ether as fictions; what would he say to Schrödinger's wave-mechanics, which involves a *six*-dimensional *sub*-ether?[7] We are not even sure that the electron, from the behavior of which so many deductions are drawn by philosophizing scientists, is a reality.[8]

We may feel that the fictions discussed so far are simply the excrescences of scientific growth, that they do not touch the foundations of science. Let us, therefore, examine these foundations, the fundamental concepts of science, to see whether they can clear themselves of the suspicion of fiction.

Mathematics will again be the best starting point. What are the fundamentals of this science? As soon as we begin to think about this question, we realize that we are in a field of imagination, not of "fact." In geometry we find points without extension, perfectly straight lines without breadth or depth, perfect circles—none of these things is encountered in physical nature. Even the numbers, if we think of them in the abstract, seem mysterious and contradictory.[9]

In the physical sciences we deal with certain fundamental conceptions, such as energy, matter, space, and time. Everyone is familiar with the contradictions that seem to be in-

[7] Eddington, *The Nature of the Physical World* (1929), p. 211.

[8] "It is still questioned whether many of the objects of the most valuable and indispensable hypotheses in present use have actual existence; the existential status of the electron is still, for example, a matter of controversy." Dewey, *The Quest for Certainty* (1929), p. 191.

[9] "The Roman notation for numbers had no symbol for zero, and probably most mathematicians of the ancient world would have been horribly puzzled by the idea of the number zero. For, after all, it is a very subtle idea, not at all obvious. A great deal of discussion on the meaning of the zero of quantity will be found in philosophic works. Zero is not, in real truth, more difficult or subtle in idea than the other cardinal numbers. What do we mean by 1, or by 2, or by 3? But we are familiar with the use of these ideas, though we should most of us be puzzled to give a clear analysis of the simpler ideas which go to form them." Whitehead, *An Introduction to Mathematics* (n.d.), p. 63.

volved in the notions of space and time. But matter and energy may seem more substantial. What is the physicist's definition of matter? "That which may have energy communicated to it from other matter, and which may in its turn communicate energy to other matter." What, then, is energy? "Energy [is] that which in all natural phenomena is continually passing from one portion of matter to another."[10] We are back where we started. Our definitions are circular, our explanations tautological.

The fundamental assumptions of any science, when closely examined, prove illusory and often contradictory. The lawyer cannot formulate a clear, general distinction between "law" and "fact," though this distinction would seem to be fundamental to his science. Again, we say that a man may sue a trespasser because he is the owner of the land trespassed upon, and that the law "protects his ownership" by giving him an action. Asked for a definition of his ownership, we respond by saying that it is a "bundle of rights," including the right to sue for trespass. He can sue because he is owner; he is owner because he can sue.

A French writer[11] refers to the legal fiction as proceeding from an intellectual lassitude comparable to that of the physicists of the seventeenth and eighteenth centuries who explained a well-known phenomenon by saying that "nature abhors a vacuum." He urges that the law follow the example of science, which has given up this metaphor for the true explanation, that of atmospheric pressure. But what is atmospheric pressure? Is the notion that the atmosphere "presses" any more satisfactory than the rejected metaphor? We say, of course, that "atmospheric pressure" as experienced on the earth's surface is but a way of describing the

---

[10] The definitions are those of Clerk-Maxwell, and are quoted from Pearson, *The Grammar of Science* (3d ed., 1911), p. 272.

[11] Lecocq, *De la fiction comme procédé juridique* (1914), p. 242.

effect of the gravitational pull of the earth on the air. But, again, what is this "pull" of gravity? Newton himself realized that no explanation was to be found in the idea of an "attraction" or "pull"; indeed, he regarded the idea of an "attraction" operating through empty space as absurd.[12] Modern physicists, in their effort to get away from "anthropomorphic" conceptions, are leaving out the metaphoric "pull." Some now define gravitation prosaically as a "property of space." Unsatisfying to the layman as this explanation may seem, we feel at least that it is not fictitious. But is this true? We have here a fundamental category of thought, that of the Thing and its Properties. We regard space as an entity, and gravitation as one of its "qualities" or "attributes." And yet this notion of the Thing and its Properties, fundamental as it is for thought, is tautological and fictitious. How can we define the thing, except in terms of its properties? We say that sugar (the *thing*) has the *property* of being sweet, white, dissoluble, etc. But when we come to define the *thing* (sugar), we simply enumerate its most important *properties*. The properties *are* the thing, yet we regard them as appurtenances *to* the thing, as if the thing were something more than the sum total of its properties.[13]

[12] "You sometimes speak of gravity as essential and inherent to matter. Pray do not ascribe that notion to me; for the cause of gravity is what I do not pretend to know. . . . That gravity should be innate, inherent and essential to matter, so that one body may act upon another at a distance through a vacuum, without the mediation of any thing else, by and through which their action and force may be conveyed from one to another, is to me so great an absurdity, that I believe no man who has in philosophical matters a competent faculty of thinking, can ever fall into it." From Newton's letters to Bentley, quoted from Mach, p. 237.

[13] "At the same time our categories may be *shifted* in the sense that that which we have just treated as a property may itself in turn be reified and regarded as a carrier of qualities. Thus we say not only, 'Sugar is sweet,' but also, 'Sweetness has the property of making food tasteful.'" Mallachow, *Rechtserkenntnistheorie und Fiktionslehre* (1922), p. 21.

All of these notions which we have successively employed in explaining the effect of a vacuum—the abhorrence of nature for a vacuum, the "pressure" of the atmosphere, the "pull" of gravity, the appurtenance of gravity to space—are in reality only "an empty reduplication of the fact of a succession of relationships."[14]

The most elementary thought cannot proceed without classifications, yet Vaihinger regards classifications as fictions. They are fictions for two distinct reasons. (1) We treat the class as a distinct entity, though it is composed of individuals that vary among themselves. We speak of the class "man," though it is impossible to think of a man in the abstract. If we visualize a man, he must be black or white, short or tall. Yet our abstract man must be a black-white, short-tall man. (2) "Natural" classes rarely, if ever, exist. We are constantly encountering borderline cases which upset our classifications. We were beginning to feel that "man" formed a natural class when someone dug up Pithecanthropus erectus. Even those qualities which seem so opposed that they are used as synonyms for the idea of contrast—black and white, life and death—shade into one another by imperceptible degrees.

In the field of morality and ethics we encounter the same difficulties. We are unable to pass moral judgment on the conduct of others without the assumption of free will, an assumption which contradicts our belief that "cause and effect rule the universe." The assumption of free will is even worse than that; it is self-contradictory. A completely "free" action would seem to be as much beyond the pale of moral criticism or approval as a mechanically "caused" action.[15]

---

[14] Ellis, p. 90.

[15] "Actions are, by their very nature, temporary and perishing; and where they proceed not from some *cause* in the character and disposition of the person who performed them, they can neither redound to his honour, if good; nor infamy, if evil. The actions themselves may be blameable; they may be contrary to all the rules of morality and reli-

We are now ready to repeat Vaihinger's question: *How does it come about that with consciously false ideas we are yet able to reach conclusions that are right?*

Vaihinger's Answer

A question may frequently be unanswerable and, indeed, meaningless, because it tacitly assumes something that is false. Vaihinger found that to be the case here. The difficulty was not in *answering* the question; it lay deeper. The trouble arose out of the assumptions that were made in *asking* the question.

We say we reach "right" results by proceeding upon "false" ideas. But why do we believe these ideas to be "false"? What is the standard by which we determine their "falsity"? Is it not clear, on reflection, that we have been determining "truth" or "falsity" by the inquiry: Has the idea in question a counterpart in the world of reality external to us? We talk of "energy," yet we cannot find a single thing in the universe that is "energy" and nothing else; therefore "energy" is a false notion. We talk of points without extension, yet we cannot find them in nature; therefore mathematical points are fictions. This lack of a physical counterpart for our intellectual processes is the thing that has led us to call our ideas "false." But whence comes this notion that our ideas must have physical counterparts in nature? What justifies the assumption we have been making that our minds should be like mirrors, reflecting nature in miniature?

Our minds are not mere passive reflectors of the external world; they are instruments for enabling us to deal with that

---

gion: But the person is not answerable for them; and as they proceeded from nothing in him that is durable and constant, and leave nothing of that nature behind them, it is impossible he can, upon their account, become the object of punishment or vengeance." Hume, *An Enquiry Concerning Human Understanding* (1777), the section "Of Liberty and Necessity."

world. As instruments is it any wonder that they *alter* reality? The whole human body is an elaborate machine for altering the environment in which we are placed. The food we eat is subjected to an elaborate process of chemical alteration before it is absorbed into our bodies. The sound waves that strike our ears are not transmitted directly to the brain, but undergo a complicated process of modification and reproduction before stimulating the sensation of sound. If the principle of alteration applies to other bodily processes, is it not natural that it should also apply to the mind? "Just as the physical organism breaks up the matter which it receives and mixes it with its own secretions, thus preparing it for assimilation, so the mind envelops the thing perceived with categories which it has developed out of itself."[16] "The mind is not merely receptive, it is appropriative and elaborative."[17]

If the alteration that reality undergoes in our minds is called "falsification," it is because we have been proceeding upon an erroneous theory of truth, a theory that we may call "the picture theory of truth." If we regard the matter in its true light, this alteration of reality is a sign not of the weakness of the human intellect but rather of its strength. If we dealt with reality as it is, in its crude, unorganized form, we should be helpless. Instead of that, our minds have the capacity for altering, simplifying, rearranging reality. This process of elaboration and alteration is—to preserve the organic simile—but the sign of a good mental digestion; it indicates the vigor and capacity of our minds.

[16] Vaihinger, p. 3.

[17] *Ibid.* "It is not correspondence with a supposed 'objective reality' (which in any event is said not to be directly accessible to us), it is not the theoretic 'duplication' of the outer world in the mirror of consciousness, nor yet a speculative comparison of the products of thought with objective things which, in our view, furnishes assurance that thought has fulfilled its purpose; it is rather the *practical* test, *whether it is possible with the help of these products of thought to calculate those events which occur without our intervention, and to carry into successful effect our desires under the guidance of these logical constructs*" (p. 5). (Italics in the original.)

If we discard the picture theory of truth and recognize that the world of ideas is intended not as a counterfeit of external reality but as an instrument which enables us to orient ourselves in this world of reality, we shall see that science has two tasks: (1) to determine the successions and interrelations of the events of the external world, and (2) to organize the concepts through which we express and make understandable these successions and interrelations into a form as neat, adequate, useful, and innocuous as possible.[18] This will carry with it the implication that there may be several "right" solutions for a given problem, just as there may be, in different animals, different organic structures serving essentially the same purpose.

If the new physics has brought its own perplexities in the form of apparently absurd notions which nevertheless seem to be productive and useful, it has also done much to bring scientists to a realization of the true purpose of intellectual constructs. It has quite generally and frankly adopted the "as if" attitude.[19] Nor are signs lacking that a similar attitude is being adopted in other sciences.[20]

[18] *Ibid.,* p. 97.

[19] The following quotations from Eddington are illustrative of the adoption of the "as if" attitude in modern science: "I have been encouraging you to think of space-time as curved; but I have been careful to speak of this as a picture, not as a hypothesis" (p. 157). "In Bohr's semi-classical model of the hydrogen atom there is an electron describing a circular or elliptic orbit. This is only a model; the real atom contains nothing of the sort. The real atom contains something which it has not entered into the mind of man to conceive" (p. 199). "The square root of -1 ... is only a well-known subterfuge" (p. 208). "Schrödinger's wave-mechanics is not a physical theory but a dodge—and a very good dodge too" (p. 219).

In a passage already quoted in part, Dewey says, "It is still questioned whether many of the objects of the most valuable and indispensable hypotheses in present use have actual existence. ... In many cases, as in the older theory of the nature of atoms, it is now clear that their worth was independent of the existential status imputed to their subject-matter; that indeed this imputation was irrelevant and as far as it went injurious." *The Quest for Certainty,* p. 191.

[20] One modern psychologist, for example, conceives the problem of psychology to be the "task of finding *productive assumptions* about the

If we cease to view thought as an attempt to "reproduce" reality and conceive of it as a process of reducing reality to a form our minds can absorb, then to understand thought we must examine in detail the procedures through which this alteration takes place. We shall find that there are two main processes of alteration. *First,* there is the process of simplification and organization, and *second,* there is the process of converting new experiences into familiar terms.[21] A more detailed analysis of these processes will next be in order.

The Process of Simplification and Organization

The most obvious example of the process by which our minds simplify reality is to be found in what Vaihinger calls "neglective fictions." "I group together under the heading [abstractive or neglective fictions] a series of methods in which the deviation from reality manifests itself specifically as a disregard of certain elements in the fact situation."[22]

The assumption of some economists, that man is an "economic animal" constantly seeking his own advantage, is an illustration of this sort of fiction.[23] In a field where conduct is determined by the interplay of a large number of factors,

---

hidden parts of behavior." Köhler, *Gestalt Psychology* (1929), p. 54, italics mine. Many psychologists regard the "unconscious" (as a separate entity) merely as a convenience in description and explanation. See Rueff, *From the Physical to the Social Sciences* (1929), p. 73.

21 This twofold division is not to be found in Vaihinger, but seems to me to be implicit in his discussion.

22 Vaihinger, p. 28.

23 See Vaihinger's discussion of Adam Smith's economic method, pp. 341 *et seq.* The assumption is false in two particulars: (1) it ignores the fact of altruism in human nature, and (2) it ignores the fact that human beings often, perhaps generally, act from mere habit and custom without considering the effect of their actions upon their own interests. Of course, whether the notion of man as an "economic animal" is properly called a "fiction" is largely a question of terminology. Cf. Professor Cohen's discussion of this notion in the article "On the Logic of Fiction," 20 *Jour. of Philos.* (1923), 477, 482. If one's primary object is to warn against a *misuse* of such notions, the term "fiction" has an undeniable utility.

artificial abstraction is necessary. Progress cannot be made without the conscious disregard of minor factors. These "neglective fictions" are especially useful in psychology and the social sciences.[24]

The "laws" developed through the use of neglective assumptions are often simplificatory falsifications of reality, exceedingly useful for some purposes, and highly dangerous when employed for ends not in the mind of the scientist who developed them. When one sets about consciously to disregard certain factors in a complex situation, one must keep constantly in mind the end toward which one is working. The question, what factors may safely be disregarded, depends necessarily upon the purpose for which the neglective assumption is being developed. One must guard against an unjustified transference of assumptions, which may be useful and productive in one field, to another field in which the factors neglected by the assumption assume a primary importance. The fiction that man is an "economic animal" has great utility when one's problem is to develop laws of economic behavior; taken as a foundation for ethics it would be disastrous. For certain purposes it is useful to exclude the field of morality from that of law. But again, the separation must be regarded as provisional only. It must not be taken for a permanent reality.[25]

---

[24] "*Artificial simplification or abstraction is a necessary precondition of securing ability to deal with affairs which are complex, in which there are many more variables and where strict isolation destroys the special characteristics of the subject-matter.*" This statement conveys the important distinction which exists between physical and social and moral objects. The distinction is one of methods of operation not of kinds of reality." Dewey, *The Quest for Certainty*, p. 217.

[25] Vaihinger says that many jurists (for example, Binding) regard the relation of law and morals as that of two circles which do not intersect, so that each field is entirely exclusive of the other. While this separation may have great value for certain purposes, one should not forget that there lies at the foot of it an "as if," and that the separation is tentative and conditioned by the end in view. "This remark is of im-

The device of legal technique that bears the closest resemblance to Vaihinger's neglective fiction is the prima facie presumption. Through the use of presumptions the law confers
upon facts a clarity of outline lacking in nature. The presumption introduces into an entangled mass of interrelated
events a certain tractable simplicity without which the effective administration of justice would be impossible.[26] Not only
does the presumption have the same utility as the neglective
fiction of science; it is also subject to the same abuses. A
caution against unjustified transference is as necessary in the
law as it is in science.[27]

But the process of simplification and organization is not
confined to the rather obvious method of the neglective
fiction. The categories of thought serve a similar purpose.
The category of the Thing and its Properties, tautological as
it is, is a device for organizing and simplifying reality to a
condition suitable to our needs. "Thought creates imagina-
tively a 'thing,' and then tacks to this thing its own perceptions as 'properties'; with the aid of this fiction the mind
works itself out of the sea of invading sensations."[28] "We can

---

portance because, through a lack of methodological insight, the case is
not infrequent in which jurists have regarded this fiction [of the complete separation of law and morality] as the real relation—a grievous
and disastrous mistake" (p. 375).

[26] "The affairs of mankind would fall into an inextricable confusion
leading to dismay and evil if the rules of evidence were not [in certain
cases] relaxed and if the law did not delight in applying certain kindly
and convenient presumptions." Lamm, J., in *Hartwell* v. *Parks* (1912)
240 Mo. 537, 545, 144 S.W. 793, 795.

[27] For example, it may be safe to presume that a woman of advanced
years is incapable of bearing children in a case where the improbable
event of the birth of a child would not upset property rights, and unsafe
to make a similar presumption where the unexpected event would
operate to throw a series of estates into confusion. See the note in *18
Harv. L. Rev.* (1905), 545. In determining the question whether it is
wise to disregard the possibility of an event that is improbable, we must
keep in mind what the effect of the event's happening would be in the
particular case.

[28] Vaihinger, p. 305.

only regard reality as a Heraclitean flux of happening, and our thinking itself would be fluid and would run together if it were not that by fiction we obtain imaginary standpoints and boundaries by which we gain control over the flow of reality."[29]

The postulating of "classes" is another illustration of the same process of simplification and organization. This procedure (that of "classifying") also illustrates another important point—that most of this simplification and organization takes place without our being aware of it. Language does a great deal of this labor for us almost automatically. We can only appreciate this service when we consider what the situation would be if we were deprived of speech as an organizing and classifying power. We get some hint of this when we consider primitive languages. The grammars and classifications of primitive languages are often unbelievably complex. In a dialect of British Columbia there are no fewer than seven different sets of counting words, choice between them being determined by the nature of the objects counted.[30] We find striking hiatuses in primitive languages; there may be a separate word for each phase of the moon, but no word for "moon" in general, a word for each separate kind of fish, but no word for the class "fish."[31] In the words of Vaihinger, "It

[29] *Ibid.*, p. 411.
[30] There is a separate set for flat objects, for round objects, for men, for long objects, for boats, for units of measure, and a final set for objects not falling within one of these classes. Lévy-Bruhl, *How Natives Think* (1926), p. 194; *Les fonctions mentales dans les sociétés inférieures* (1910), p. 223.
[31] "If the average man who had not looked into the matter at all were asked to say what sort of language he imagined a savage to have, he would be pretty sure to reply that in the first place the vocabulary would be very small, and in the second place it would consist of very short, comprehensive terms—roots, in fact—such as 'man,' 'bear,' 'eat,' 'kill,' and so on. Nothing of the sort is actually the case. Take the inhabitants of that cheerless spot, Tierra del Fuego, whose culture is as rude as that of any people on earth. A scholar who tried to put together a dictionary of their language found that he had got to reckon with more

should be emphasized that an indefinite number of such categories [of thought] can be conceived. One may affirm that originally the mind possessed a much richer table of categories than today, and that the present table of categories is only the product of a process of natural selection and adaptation."[32]

Because the process of language-learning takes place in the years of infancy, we easily forget the service language does to thought. As Mach has pointed out, as soon as we are really capable of critical self-observation, we find already developed in ourselves a conceptual apparatus for classifying the external world.[33]

Vaihinger deals chiefly with the simplificatory and formative processes of the "higher" mental faculties, i.e., with those processes that take place in the mental regions available to introspective examination. He recognizes the possibility, however, that much organization and simplification may occur in the "lower" mental regions, i.e., in "sensation" and

---

than thirty thousand words, even after suppressing a large number of forms of lesser importance. And no wonder that the tally mounted up. For the Fuegians had more than twenty words, some containing four syllables, to express what for us would be either 'he' or 'she'; then they had two names for the sun, two for the moon, and two more for the full moon, each of the last-named containing four syllables and having no element in common." R. R. Marett, *Anthropology* (n.d.), pp. 138–39. We find in our own language hangovers from an earlier period in such lists as flock, herd, covey, drove, swarm, shoal, band, etc.

32 Vaihinger, p. 313. He is of course using the term "category" in its philosophical sense as a "frame of thought." But that does not mar the pertinence of his remarks in our present connection.

33 *Die Analyse der Empfindungen und das Verhältniss des Physischen zum Psychischen* (3d ed., 1902), p. 240. Cf. "The world of our experience must be enormously simplified and generalized before it is possible to make a symbolic inventory of all our experiences of things and relations; and this inventory is imperative before we can convey ideas. . . . Only so is communication possible, for the single experience lodges in an individual consciousness and is, strictly speaking, incommunicable. To be communicated it needs to be referred to a class which is tacitly accepted by the community as an identity." Sapir, *Language* (1921), p. 11.

"perception."[34] Modern psychology has, from its beginnings, recognized the formative process involved in perception.[35] Gestalt psychology has made this "configuratory" process the very core of its theory. One of the experiments of this school is worth reporting here.

Imagine twelve small white disks against a black background, arranged in such a way that the disks, if joined together by straight lines, would form a regular twelve-sided figure. Now alter this pattern so that any one of the disks is somewhat farther from the center of the figure than the other eleven disks. This alteration has of course destroyed the symmetry of the figure; the pattern now appears to you to be out of balance. If this unbalanced figure is presented for a small fraction of a second a strange thing will be seen to happen. The displaced disk shoots inward toward the position it would occupy were the figure to become a regular, simple, balanced one. Of course, no motion has occurred in the physical sense of that word, but nevertheless the illusion of motion is experienced.[36]

The inveterate hang of the human mind toward an organized simplicity—so deep-seated, we have just seen, as to invade even the elementary processes of sensation and perception—has been of great value to the human race in the struggle for existence. But, like every valuable faculty, it is subject

[34] Vaihinger, pp. 286, 297. Cf. Pearson's suggestion of "the mind as a sorting machine" (p. 106).

[35] "All brain-processes are such as give rise to what we may call *figured* consciousness . . . ; whilst part of what we perceive comes through our senses from the object before us, another part (and it may be the larger part) always comes out of our own mind." James, *Psychology, Briefer Course* (1917), pp. 316, 329.

[36] Squires, "A New Psychology after the Manner of Einstein," *Scientific Monthly*, February 1930, pp. 156, 161. The process of organization and simplification takes place also in memory. Memory simplifies the thing remembered, not merely in the sense that unimportant items are eliminated, but in the sense that memory seems actually to organize and "give form" to our experiences. See the experiments discussed in Köhler, pp. 307-10. Perhaps we can say that stories improve not only "in the telling" but in the remembering as well!

to abuses. It must be held in restraint; it must be exercised with judgment. We see the necessity for this particularly in dealing with classifications. The human mind seems to have an instinctive tendency to conceive of classifications in geometric terms; we tend to suppose that the members of a class are of equal importance, and that the interrelations between them must form a balanced, geometric pattern. The recent history of American legal thought offers an example of this tendency. When the Hohfeldian system was first announced, it seemed to throw so much light on hitherto darkened corners of legal analysis, it offered so much hope for a rational and clear expression of legal relations, that we felt we had at last discovered the atomic system which lay at the heart of legal thought. It was assumed that the whole set of Hohfeldian relations must form a geometric figure, and that much knowledge could be gained merely by manipulating the table, by arranging the elements into "opposites," "correlatives," etc. It was some time before we realized that the four pillars of this system are, unfortunately for symmetry, of rather unequal height and importance, and that very little is to be gained through a mere manipulation of the tables of "jural relations."[37]

[37] It would hardly be questioned today that the early exponents of the Hohfeldian system overemphasized the importance of the "privilege-no-right" relationship. In describing the legal situation of a given individual, I can recite "privilege-no-right" relations indefinitely; "he is privileged to stand on his head," "to put a feather in his hat," etc. Only certain of my statements will have any real legal significance, will describe in the words of Dean Pound ("Legal Rights," *26 Int. Jour. of Ethics* [1915], 92) "significant legal institutions." The same thing cannot be said of the "right-duty" relationship. The "right-duty" pillar is a much more substantial and imposing monument than the "privilege-no-right" pillar. While it may be convenient to regard the "privilege-no-right" relation as a *legal* relation, it is important to keep in mind that its significance arises only from the possibility that a "right-duty" relation might have existed in its stead, and in that sense the significance of the "privilege-no-right" relation is always negative and derivative.

An oversimplified, geometric view of the Hohfeldian system would seem to underlie the criticism in *28 Yale L. Jour.* (1919), 387, of Jus-

New Experiences Are Converted into the Terms
of Those Already Familiar

A small boy, on seeing a horse for the first time, called it a "big dog." The child was perhaps aware that the horse represented for him an essentially new experience, but he was constrained to deal with the anomalous object in terms of that which was already familiar to him. He adopted a temporary fiction, perhaps anticipating the necessity of later correction. This simple example illustrates a very important limitation upon human knowledge, a limitation that is often forgotten. Vaihinger stresses again and again the point that human thought must always proceed by analogy, and that analogies must always be taken from an existing stock of experience.[38]

This fundamental limitation upon human thought has al-

---

tice Brandeis' dissenting opinion in *International News Service* v. *Associated Press* (1918) 248 U.S. 215. In that case the majority of the court upheld the right of the Associated Press to restrain the News Service from "pirating" news from the bulletins published by the Associated Press. The case was a new one, and Justice Brandeis, in his dissenting opinion, expressed the view that the problem presented was more properly a matter for legislation than for court action. In the course of developing this idea, he said that it was not a case where a court ought "to establish a new rule of law." He is criticized for this remark in the note referred to, where the view is taken that the establishment of a "privilege-no-right" relationship (which would be involved in the denial of relief) is "just as clearly" the enunciation of a "rule of law" as the establishment of a "right-duty" relation. Now one may, with much reason, take the view that a "privilege-no-right" relation is properly described as a "legal" relation, and that the declaration by a court of a "privilege" is the establishment of a rule of law. But one cannot deny that when a court begins to delimit and restrict a line of conduct, it is undertaking a very different responsibility from that involved in the mere declaration of a "hands off" policy. And many lawyers would express this difference by saying that in the first case the court was "making law," while in the second it was not. That is all Justice Brandeis meant to imply by his remarks. It is certainly questionable whether Justice Brandeis was the victim of an "illusion," as the note suggests; if any "illusion" is involved, it is probably that of the author of the note, who seems to entertain the belief that it is proper to interpret the remarks of another in the terms of one's own private definitions.

[38] "Metaphors are not merely artificial devices for making discourse more vivid and poetical, but are also necessary means for the appre-

ready been touched on in a number of places in this study. We saw it illustrated in the growth of legal language when we observed the metaphorical extension which familiar terms undergo at the hands of the law.[39] We saw it again illustrated in the legal fiction proceeding from "intellectual conservatism," the fiction through which a new case is forced into the framework of existing categories.[40]

The same thing is illustrated in all the "anthropomorphic" and metaphorical conceptions of science. Empty space is conceptually filled with ether to satisfy our feeling—derived from previous experience—that vibrations can take place only in some sort of matter. We speak of the "affinity" of chemicals for one another, of the "flow" of electricity, of the "pull" of gravity. "Scientific explanation ... in its essence, generally consists in describing new phenomena in terms of others more familiar to our minds."[41]

This process of understanding through analogies goes hand in hand with the process of simplification and organization, discussed in the last section. We feel the need of "catching-on places" in the flux of reality, and we develop (unconsciously) the category of the Thing and its Properties, we group phenomena into entities and their attributes. This is simplification and organization. But when we come to conceive of the relationship between our constructed entity and the particular perceptions out of which it is constructed, we invoke an analogy from familiar experience, that of "ownership." The thing is given "properties." Conceivably an entirely different analogy might have been hit upon. We might, for example, have spoken of the "father and his children," or of "the rose and its petals."

But, the reader may say, admitting that human reasoning

---

hension and communication of new ideas." Cohen, "On the Logic of Fiction," pp. 477, 478.

[39] *Live and Dead Fictions, supra,* pp. 14–18.
[40] *Supra,* pp. 63–70.
[41] Dampier-Whetham, *A History of Science* (1930), p. 47.

proceeds always by analogy, does this fact represent an *alteration* of reality? Vaihinger's fundamental thesis is that our minds do not merely reflect reality, but alter it and "work it over" to suit our needs. Does he establish a process of alteration by showing that reasoning proceeds by likening new experiences to those already familiar? The horse may remain in the child's mind an essentially new experience, even when it is called a dog; empty space may remain the same for the scientist after he has filled it conceptually with "ether." Does reasoning by analogy necessarily involve an alteration or distortion of reality? The answer is that it *need not,* but in practice it *generally does.* The congenital predisposition toward simplicity of the human mind leads us to give too much credence to our analogies. The child, after calling the horse a dog, may expect the horse to bark; the scientist, after calling space ether, may be misled into erroneous notions through a too implicit trust in the analogy to matter.[42] The lawyer, after calling the corporation a "person," may assume that the corporation, like the human being, must die, "all at once," and that at any given point of time the corporation must be either "alive" or "dead."[43] *A metaphorical element taints all our concepts.*

---

[42] "Just as we were misled into untenable ideas of the ether through trusting to an analogy with the material ocean, so we have been misled into untenable ideas of the attributes of the microscopic elements of world-structure through trusting to analogy with gross particles." Eddington, p. 225.

[43] An insight into the nature of concepts ought to tell one that the "existence" of a corporation consists in the attribution of certain capacities and liabilities to a constructed entity, and that certain of these capacities and liabilities may be removed, while others remain. There is no violation of good methodology or common sense in saying that the corporation continues to "exist" for some purposes after it has ceased to "exist" for others. (See *The Life Association of America* v. *Fassett* [1882] 102 Ill. 315, 324.) But this free and easy way of thought has not always been in vogue. Cf. "Now the effect of dissolution . . . is, that . . . the corporation is wholly gone, and with it are also lost and avoided all its claims, debts, and liabilities of all kinds." Grant, *The Law of Corporations* (1854), *303.

Metaphorical contamination is at a minimum in mathematical symbols. It is perhaps negligible in certain other concepts. Many of our familiar analogies have come to have, at least for the scientist, the colorless quality of mathematical symbols. The ether becomes merely an intellectual concept "solely useful for the purpose of describing our perceptual routine."[44] The "laws" of nature, often conceived of by the layman as, in some mysterious way, "ruling the universe," become for the scientist merely "limitations which, under the guidance of experience, we impose on our expectations."[45] Our metaphors and fictions are dying. In the words of Vaihinger, they are becoming "verbal" or "nominal" fictions.[46]

But few of them are completely dead. If in the case of some scientific concepts, and for some investigators, metaphorical contamination has been reduced to a point approximating the mathematical symbol, in most of our concepts, this metaphorical element remains dangerously active. This is particularly true in the social sciences, where the complexity of the fact-situation emphasizes and stimulates the human penchant for simplicity.

Vaihinger's Precept for the Use of Fictions

There is perhaps no more suggestive part of Vaihinger's book than that in which he attempts to formulate a precept for the application of fictions, a rule that will prevent their misuse.[47] Here, as often, he takes his illustration from mathe-

---

[44] Pearson, p. v.

[45] Mach, *Erkenntnis und Irrtum,* p. 449.

[46] It may be said that Vaihinger fails to recognize sufficiently the possibility that certain fictions are "dead." He seems frequently to think that a fictional element is present in a concept if it can be demonstrated etymologically. He never recognizes explicitly the development we have called the death of the fiction, a notion that may not be entirely lacking in epistemological significance.

[47] Vaihinger, pp. 194–219.

matics. The mathematician sometimes finds that he may simplify the solution of an equation by inserting into it, provisionally, a foreign element. This foreign element may be
retained through a series of calculations. But—and here is
the important point—the mathematician must not forget to
remove it before he reaches his final result. *The fiction must
drop out of the final reckoning.* This is the precept that
Vaihinger sets up for the use of the fiction.

We may group phenomena together into convenient units
of thought, treat the constructed entity as a "thing," and attribute to it as "properties" the elements out of which it is
composed. The "thing" represents the introduction of a foreign element into our equation which may serve to facilitate
our calculations. But the fiction (the "thing") must drop out
of the final reckoning; we must not suppose that the "thing"
is something more than the sum-total of its properties. If, in
physics, the scientist divides a succession of relationships into
two distinct entities, "matter" and "energy," he must not forget to reconnect these two entities "in the final reckoning";
he must remember that the separation was provisional only
and for the purpose of facilitating computation. He must not
conceive of energy as something that can exist distinct from
matter, or of matter as something that can exist distinct from
energy.

This dropping of the fiction from the final reckoning Vaihinger calls "the correction of a previous, intentional error."
We find this process illustrated in many fields of the law.[48]
We call the corporation a person. This statement is false; it
represents the introduction of a foreign element into our
calculations, the notion of the "personality" of the corporation. But we correct the error by extracting from the word

---

[48] Vaihinger's own statement (p. 197) that such a correction is not
necessary in the case of legal fictions can only be attributed to his lack
of an intimate acquaintance with the legal fiction.

"person" (when it is applied to corporations) all those qualities and attributes not legally appropriate to the corporation. The reader will have realized that the process of linguistic development by which fictions "die" is but the outward expression of the application of Vaihinger's correction. In truth we may say, a fiction is dead when the majority of persons have learned to make the necessary correction intuitively.

Vaihinger points out that much of our thinking consists in the process of opposing mistakes which are mutually compensatory. If the mathematician supposes a curve to be made of straight lines, he makes his mistake harmless by supposing in turn that the straight lines are infinitely short. Vaihinger likens thought to the process of walking. Walking consists of a series of falls, each arresting and compensating the other just in time. So thinking consists in a series of mutually opposed mistakes.[49]

That original sin of human reasoning—hypostatization— is a failure to drop the fiction out of the final reckoning.

---

[49] The statement that thinking consists of a series of compensatory errors must not be taken too literally. Like all other scientific explanations, it is only a metaphor which gives insight. The "as if" attitude must be preserved, and, indeed, becomes particularly appropriate, when one is dealing with the phenomena of internal mental experience. We can imperfectly and metaphorically describe thinking by supposing that it consists of a comparison of a series of "pictures," or that it consists of talking to one's self, or—as Vaihinger does—that it consists of a series of mutually opposed errors. None of these descriptions is completely "true"; it is a question merely of which is the most useful.

Even the syllogism, so much abused in current legal writings, has its utility as a description of internal mental experience. Admitting that no one thinks in syllogisms, is not the syllogism a useful *approximation* of thought? Is it not a convenient fiction to talk *as if* we thought in syllogisms, instead of trying to reproduce what is essentially incommunicable, the "real" thought process? An interesting defense of the syllogism may be found in Rueff, p. 12, a study of methodology in practically all fields of science except that of the law. (The English translation was published in 1929 by the Johns Hopkins Institute for the Study of Law.) Rueff speaks of the "enormous advantage" of stating reasoning "in the form of a chain of syllogisms." "It localizes doubt. It shows us where to look for contradictions."

Or, stated differently, it consists in the isolation of one step in a reasoning process out of its compensatory context. In its context it is harmless, because it is there subjected to the corrective effect of other elements in the same process. But when a single step in a process of reasoning is removed from its corrective background and given a value on its own account, the inevitable result is intellectual disaster. The man who tries to take a single step with the vigor and energy that go into the process of running will find himself thrown forcibly to the ground. The isolation of either a concept or a muscular contraction from its compensatory context is dangerous.[50]

Most of the "mysteries" of science and philosophy are the result of this process of isolation.[51] Negative numbers, regarded in the abstract, seem strange and absurd. What is -5? Who ever dealt with, or can even conceive of, -5 objects? And yet there is nothing mysterious about subtraction *as an operation*. If we put -5 back in its context, we find that it at once loses its mystery and becomes a sign for this operation. It is as if we were to take a single instrument out of a line of machines in a plant operating on the principle of mass production, where each separate machine performs only one step in an intricate process. Such a machine, in isolation, would seem mysterious; contemplating it alone, we might conclude that it was the product of a madman's fancy. But as soon as we put it back in its position in the line, it becomes understandable. The contradictions and difficulties that seem inherent in space and time, energy and matter,

[50] "Objection comes in, and comes in with warranted force, when the results of an abstractive operation are given a standing which belongs only to the total situation from which they have been selected." Dewey, *The Quest for Certainty*, p. 217.

[51] "The supposed 'riddle of the universe' will never be solved, because most of what appears puzzling to us consists in contradictions of our own making which arise from trifling with the mere forms and shells of understanding." Vaihinger, p. 52.

legal rights and duties, are produced by isolating what is essentially only a step in a complicated process of reasoning.

Hypostatization, or the isolation of a process of thought from a compensatory context, is bad enough when it results in mystifying and perplexing the mind. It becomes even more vicious when the isolated element is given a value on its own account and is used as a point of departure for other reasoning processes. For example, the notion of "unity" or "identity" has no meaning out of a complete context of thought-operations. "Unity" and "identity" are matters of subjective convenience. Conceptually one may postulate entities wherever it is convenient to do so.[52] Whether a given group of phenomena or experiences should be formed into a "unit" can never be determined by reference to the notion of "unity" itself. Yet the attempt to do this is a common mistake in legal thinking. In dealing with the law of fixtures and the question when a chattel "becomes a part of the soil," many courts have regarded their problem as essentially one of discovery, to "find out" when and under what circumstances a chattel and the land form a "unit" or "become one." They have failed to see that "unity" or "oneness" is a mere frame of thought, having no content of itself. I can, *conceptually*, "annex to the land" a rabbit bounding across it as fast as his legs will carry him; *conceptually*, I can "sever from the soil" a machine weighing tons. Whether I shall employ the one conception or the other depends upon circumstances outside the conception itself.[53]

[52] Lévy-Bruhl's much discussed "law of participation" (that in the primitive mind "objects, beings, phenomena can be . . . both themselves and something other than themselves") seems to mean no more than that primitives postulate inefficient entities upon the basis of superficial resemblances. This law is discussed in his book *How Natives Think*.

[53] The failure to realize this leads to the notion that the law of fixtures is in a state of "irreconcilable conflict." A court may in one case

Vaihinger's precept, that the fiction must drop out of the final reckoning, applies to the use of any sort of concept. Our concepts ("title," "legal right," "energy") are the constructs of our minds which facilitate thought by rendering comparison en masse possible. As all thinking proceeds through analogy and comparison, thought will be speeded up if we can group related phenomena into units convenient for comparison. But these constructs must be used as *instruments* of thought only; we must treat them as servants to be discharged as soon as they have fulfilled their functions. They are foreign elements which may be inserted into the equation provisionally to render computation simpler, but which must be dropped from the final reckoning.

The concept "title" is a useful device of legal thought and expression. It would probably be impossible to dispense with it. If we did attempt to eliminate it, probably some other expression by a process of metaphorical extension would rapidly take its place. But the concept "title" has its abuses. For example, in those cases where the problem of the law is to distribute the "rights of ownership" between two individuals (as in the cases of the mortgage and the conditional sale), it is clear that the concept "title" must be dropped out of the reckoning. "Title" is a convenient cover for the "rights of ownership" when one is dealing with them as a whole. But when one's task necessitates breaking

---

declare a chattel to have become "a part of the soil," and then in a later case (where the facts of annexation are the same but the legal issues are different) declare the chattel *not* to have become "a part of the soil." To one who hypostatizes the concept "unity," these cases will seem irreconcilable. But if one realizes that the notion of "unity" is only a frame of thought and examines the cases with a view to discovering the factors that actually lead to a difference in result, the supposed "inconsistency" and "conflict" of the cases will, to a large extent, disappear. See Bingham, "Some Suggestions Concerning the Law of Fixtures," 7 *Col. L. Rev.* (1907), 1.

through the cover and apportioning the contents among different individuals, the cover should be thrown away.[54]

Why do concepts tend to gain a value on their own account which is not legitimately coming to them as mere instruments of thought? The explanation lies in part in the inveterate hang of the human mind toward simplicity. We tend to group phenomena into as large "lumps" as possible. A concept has a kind of centripetal force by which it seeks to clear the field of anomalies and exceptions. This is at least a part of the explanation. It may be supplemented, on the psychological side, by the following quotation from Mach:

> The serviceable and valuable habit of giving a name to that which is stable and constant [in a group of phenomena] and of grouping these stable elements together in one thought ... may, at times, result in a peculiar conflict with the tendency to separate these elements. The dim picture of that which is constant, which is not noticeably altered when one or the other of the elements is removed, seems to be something in and of itself. Because one may take each of the elements of the concept singly away, without this picture ceasing to represent the whole complex, ... one concludes that one might take away all the elements and there would still be something left.[55]

Eddington's view, that the concepts of physics are only ways of grouping together series of "pointer readings," has become familiar. But Eddington recognizes that many will not be satisfied with this way of looking at the thing and will want to attribute more "substance" to their concepts.

> You may if you like think of mass as something of inscrutable nature to which the pointer reading has a kind of relevance. But in physics at least there is nothing much to be gained by this mystification, because it is the pointer

---

[54] See Sturges and Clark, "Legal Theory and Real Property Mortgages," 37 Yale L. Jour. (1928), 691.

[55] Die Analyse der Empfindungen, p. 5.

reading itself which is handled in exact science; and if you imbed it in something of a more transcendental nature, you have only the extra trouble of digging it out again.[56]

If one were to attempt to generalize about the dangers of concepts, one might distinguish (1) their centripetal force; (2) their capacity for inducing reification; and (3) their metaphorical contamination. The centripetal force of the concept (the tendency, for example, to conclude that if a man has "title" for one purpose, he must have it for all purposes) proceeds from the penchant of the human mind for an organized simplicity. The capacity of the concept for inducing reification (the tendency, for example, to suppose that a corporation would still legally "exist" if one were to take away all of its legal rights, duties and entitlements) is produced by isolating a reasoning process from its context. The metaphorical contamination of a concept (the tendency in the law, for example, to be influenced by the literal meanings of words like "delivery," "conversion," "implied," and "reversion") arises from the fact that human reason proceeds by assimilating new experiences under familiar categories.

Criticisms of Vaihinger

A very common criticism of Vaihinger is to say that he proves too much. If everything is "fiction," then the meaning of the word "fiction" has been lost, and "as if" has become simply "is." Indeed, uncharitable critics have not been wanting who were willing to suggest that if everything is fiction, then this includes Vaihinger's own philosophy, and we may safely neglect to bother our heads about it unless we happen to have a taste for fantasy.[57] But a truer criticism of Vaihin-

[56] *The Nature of the Physical World*, p. 255.
[57] "If, as Vaihinger contends, there is no such thing as truth, then his own 'philosophy' . . . has no truth and represents only the idle play of the wit and ingenuity of its founder." Drews, *Geschichte der Philosophie* (1921), VIII, 95.

ger would seem to be, not that he proved too much, but that he never fully realized *what* he had proved. There runs through the whole book a curious double language. He speaks of the "illusion of knowledge" produced by the fiction and at the same time recognizes that this knowledge is real in the sense that it enables us to deal with reality and is in fact the only knowledge we ever knew or can know. He speaks constantly of "falsifying reality," and yet recognizes that the use of the word "falsifying" is a retention of the very notions of truth which he is combating in his book. This peculiarity may be explained as due in part to a desire to simplify his exposition and to lead up to his fundamental conception by gradual stages, and in part to the fact that his own ideas underwent a process of development in the course of writing the book.

Nor can it be said that Vaihinger ever recognizes that he has answered his own question, "How does it come about that with consciously false ideas, we yet reach results which are right?" There are evidences throughout the book that he remained mystified by the fiction himself. Perhaps this was inevitable in the case of a man who deliberately picked out for study, in a great number of fields, precisely those devices of thought which are the least understood, even by experts in those fields. For the true mystery of the fiction consists not in the fact that we can reach right results with wrong ideas, but in the fact that the human mind, in dealing with reality, is able to go so far beyond its capacity for analyzing its own processes.

Legal Fictions Compared with Scientific Fictions

Aside from the general philosophic criticisms of Vaihinger, just discussed, there have been criticisms touching specifically the legal aspects of his work. The argument of the

critics in question runs somewhat as follows: Vaihinger's
work is based almost entirely upon "scientific" fictions. The
ends and purposes of science are radically different from
those of the law. Therefore, while Vaihinger's philosophy
may have considerable significance in the field of science,
it is generally without importance for the jurist.[58]

It must be confessed that Vaihinger's own treatment of the
legal fiction is exceedingly superficial. One will learn little
about legal fictions and legal thought directly from Vaihinger. Apparently no one has contended otherwise. But it is
another thing to say that his work is of no legal significance,
and that the legal scholar, more familiar than Vaihinger with
legal fictions and legal method generally, cannot gain much
from a study of the philosophy of "As If."

The contention that Vaihinger's philosophy has no useful
application to the law proceeds upon the assumption that
there is a fundamental difference between the methods of
the law and those of the physical sciences. The substance of
the argument consists in saying that Vaihinger develops his
philosophy around the fictions of those sciences that are concerned with the discovery and description of the facts of external reality, whereas the task of the law is not to discover
the "facts" or "laws" of nature, but to establish a set of rules
for the conduct of human beings. Hence, it is contended,
while the fictions of the physical sciences are ways of describing the structure of external reality, the fictions of the

[58] Somló insists on the view that there is no similarity between the
legal fiction and the fictions of science. *Juristische Grundlehre* (2d ed.,
1927), p. 524. While he does not mention Vaihinger by name, and perhaps was not directly acquainted with his work, it is a reasonable inference that he is combating the "fictionalism" that spread into German
legal thought from Vaihinger's philosophy. Kelsen, in a somewhat modified way, insists upon the disparity of scientific and legal fictions. "Zur
Theorie der juristischen Fiktionen," p. 630. For an answer to these
criticisms, see Mallachow, "Zur Metajurisprudenz und Rechtsphilosophie," p. 664.

law, on the other hand, are only metaphorical ways of expressing rules or commands.[59]

The reader will see that this criticism cuts to the heart of an important problem. To what extent does a similarity exist between the methods of the physical scientist and those of the lawyer? To what extent is law "scientific"?[60] This obviously presents a question too broad for adequate treatment here. But it would perhaps not be out of place to trace in broad outlines a comparison between the fictions of "science" and those of the law. This comparison, while it will by no means solve the problem of the relation of law and "science," may nevertheless throw some light on the more general question.

In the first place, it is clear that one may study law objectively and descriptively—as a "scientist." Renouncing, at least provisionally, the privilege of determining what *ought* to be, one may study the legal system as it actually exists, and attempt to reduce its complex workings to a simple set

[59] "The so-called legal fiction is nothing but an abbreviatory formula by means of which a particular legal will expresses itself." Stammler, *Theorie der Rechtswissenschaft* (2d ed., 1923), p. 201.

Somló (p. 527) defines a fiction as the treating of an unreal situation as if it were real, and goes on to say that there is no possibility for "genuine" fictions in the law, because the law asserts nothing about reality at all. A legal fiction is only the metaphorical expression of a command. It is interesting to observe that Somló is led to this highly artificial view of the nature of the legal fiction by his own fiction of the nature of the law, as the command (or promise) of a sovereign. By taking his own neglective fiction seriously he is forced into a patently erroneous interpretation of the significance of the legal fiction. To some extent the same thing is true of Stammler, though it is less obvious in his case because of the abstract nature of his presentation. The view of Stammler and Somló receives some support from Vaihinger himself. See Vaihinger, pp. 257, 197, and cf. p. 250.

[60] This question has aroused considerable interest in this country. See Patterson, "Can Law Be Scientific?" 25 *Ill. L. Rev.* (1930), 121, and the various reviews of Rueff, *From the Physical to the Social Sciences*, especially 4 *So. Calif. L. Rev.* (1930), 75.

of formulas. This is what is attempted in the various theories of the "nature of law." These theories—as, for example, that the law proceeds from a "Volksgeist,"[61] or that law is "the command of a Sovereign"—have generally been, in Vaihinger's terminology, personificative, neglective fictions. They are personificative, since they seek to attribute the law to some metaphorical being; they are neglective, because they present a one-sided picture of the whole of the phenomena which associate themselves around the word "law." Even the current American "realistic" conception of law—that law is "the way judges act"—is a neglective fiction. Why not say, if one is to achieve the ultimate in realism, that law is "the way sheriffs and marshals act"? The advantage of the current "realistic" conception lies, not in the fact that it is more "true," or even more "realistic," than the other theories, but in the fact that it concentrates attention on the most significant point in the whole complex process of lawmaking and law administration.

The fictions that attempt to describe the "nature of law in general" we may call *jurisprudential fictions*. It is obvious that they represent a precise parallel to the methods of the physical scientist. They are attempts to reduce a complex reality to a simple formula, and thus render it tractable to

[61] Despite his deductive presentation, Stammler shows a keen appreciation of the "as if" attitude in his discussion of Savigny's theory. "The notion of the 'Volk' as an animated and thinking being outside us would only be scientifically justified if it were necessary in order to fashion coherently the thought of human social life." "Wesen des Rechts und der Rechtswissenschaft" in *Systematische Rechtswissenschaft*, II[8] of *Kultur der Gegenwart* (1906), p. viii. In other words, the question is not whether the Volksgeist "exists," but solely whether that notion is useful in understanding society. In another place he recognizes that the notion of the Volksgeist represents the transference of a subjective experience (of one's own consciousness) to the "Volk" as a whole, and says that this transference would only be scientifically justified if it were necessary in order to understand social life. *Rechts- und Staatstheorien der Neuzeit* (2d ed., 1925), p. 53.

calculation.[62] That they have generally been oversimplifi-
cations results rather from the complexity of the matters
dealt with than from any difference in fundamental method.

All theories of law have this in common, that they attribute
"law" to one source (to the sovereign, the legislator, custom,
the Volksgeist, the nature of man, the nature of things, a social compact, etc.) and thus introduce a unity into our conception of the law. But even when one does not subscribe
to any particular theory of the "nature of law," one is apt,
consciously or unconsciously, to embrace what Ehrlich calls
the "fiction of the unity of the law."[63] We talk constantly as
if there were a unified body of rules proceeding from somewhere, which constitute "the law." Generally this remains
only a harmless metaphor. When we say "the law provides"
so and so, we are generally able to "expand the symbol" and
say that we only mean by this phrase to express the fact that
in a certain case the courts will act in a certain way. But
often this notion of the "unity of the law" ceases to be merely a metaphorical convenience of expression and becomes a

[62] Of course, we cannot say definitely whether the impetus to these
attempts comes from the scientific desire to reduce a complex reality to
a simple formula, in order to make the problem of dealing with that
reality simpler (cf. the "economic man"), or whether it may not have
proceeded from the less praiseworthy notion that because one *word*,
"law," is used to describe a number of things, all these things must be
reducible to some common element. But even if the latter conjecture
represents correctly the motive back of these attempts to define law,
would that mean that they were unequivocally removed from the realm
of "science"? Is "science" any less infested with word-reification than
the law?

[63] Ehrlich distinguishes six major fictions of jurisprudence. "That
the bringing and defense of a suit must be supported by a rule of law,
that the judge must always deduce his decision from a rule of law, that
the state is the source of all law, that the function of jurisprudence consists exclusively in the discovery of the will of the legislator, that the
judge in the determination of the law must not go beyond the provisions
of the statute, that jurisprudence must conceive of the rules of law as
forming a unity ... all ... of these precepts have this in common—that
upon closer inspection they reveal themselves as fictions." *Die juristische
Logik* (2d ed., 1925), pp. 148–49.

basis for deduction. Professor Hohfeld, for example, deduced
from this general notion of the unity of the law the conclusion
that, where a common-law right and an equitable right conflict (as where equity will enjoin the enforcement of a legal
right), the common-law right must in reality be "invalid,"
and only an "apparent" right.[64]

[64] "Since, in any sovereign state, there must, in the last analysis, be
but a single system of *genuine law,* since the various principles and rules
of that system must be consistent with one another, and since, accordingly, all *genuine jural* relations must be consistent with one another,
two conflicting rules, the one 'legal' and the other 'equitable,' cannot be
valid at the same moment of time: one must be valid and determinative
to the exclusion of the other." *Fundamental Legal Conceptions* (1923),
p. 136. What is the source of this series of "musts"?
Similar ideas have been expressed by Professor Beale. "It is clear,
however, that there cannot be two separate and distinct laws prevailing
in the same place at the same time; and therefore in fact, whatever may
be the theory of the courts, one of the conflicting rights must be valid
and the other invalid." Beale, *A Treatise on the Conflict of Laws*
(1916), p. 151.
Professor Cook has, on the basis of a similar line of reasoning, reached
the conclusion that in those cases where a legal right may be "set aside"
in equity (as where equity will decree the cancellation of a sealed bond
secured by fraud) the " 'legal' right is not, *as a matter of genuine substantive law, valid.*" Cook, "Equitable Defenses," 32 *Yale L. Jour.*
(1923), 645, 649. He recognizes that the spurious legal right "does have
procedural effects. If the correct procedure is not used (where courts of
equity are kept distinct from courts of law, the procedural law requires
that appeal be made to a separate court, the court of chancery), the
'legal' right will be enforced *as if* it were a genuine right." (*Ibid.,* note
18.) Although Professor Cook does not explain for us what is meant by
a "genuine" right, as distinguished from an "apparent" right, his deductions seem to flow, like those of Professors Hohfeld and Beale, from the
notion that there is some inherent impossibility in a double system of
rights existing in a single system of law.
The proper approach to the problem would seem to be to inquire,
not whether the rights in question are "genuine" or spurious, but whether the concept of a right which may be set aside is a notion possessing
utility in the description of legal relations. The notion of legal rights
which are subject to being abrogated by court action is a necessary part
of any system of jurisprudence which recognizes the convenient but
probably not indispensable distinction between transactions that are
void (or are voidable by the extracurial act of the party) and those
transactions that are regarded as legally effective until formally set
aside by the decree of a court.
It is worth noting that Ehrlich (p. 123) uses the English dual system

Closely allied to *jurisprudential fictions* are what we may
call the *fictions of legal technique*. The notions of a legal
right and duty, of legal powers and liabilities, of legal personality—all of these notions are, in the Vaihingerian sense,
fictions,[65] and, what is more important in our present context,
they represent devices essentially similar to the concepts of
the physical sciences.[66] They are the devices through which
we organize and simplify our subject matter, and they cor-
respond to such notions as "energy," "matter," and "the force
of gravity" in physics.

But when we come to those naïve and transparent devices
that come first to mind when the expression "legal fiction" is
used, the likeness to the concepts of science is less obvious.
What we may call the *fictions of applied law*, such as the
fiction of finding in the action of trover, or of inviting in the
attractive nuisance cases, seem to be entirely foreign to "science." If so, it is largely because they have generally been
produced by motives that are not operative upon the scien-

---

of law (which Professors Hohfeld, Beale and Cook force into a unit)
as proof of his thesis that the notion of the unity of the law is a fiction.
(Some objection might be taken to Ehrlich's use of the term "fiction"
as applied to the conception of the unity of the law. After all, the
"unity" of the law is perhaps no more fictional than the "unity" of a
corporation, or of anything else, including the human soul, if some
psychologists are to be believed. But, like the notion of corporate entity,
the concept of the unity of the law should be regarded as a matter of
convenience in expression, not as dogma. It will frequently be found
convenient to "pierce the veil" of the unity of the law, just as it is convenient to get behind every other kind of unity at times.)

[65] It would perhaps be better not to follow Vaihinger's example in
calling these constructs (legal right, legal person, etc.) "fictions." While
the exact boundaries of the concept "fiction" are certainly indefinite, the
word has a certain utility which would be utterly destroyed if one were
to make it equivalent with "concept" or "intellectual construct."

[66] This is recognized in Kelsen, "Zur Theorie der juristischen Fiktionen," pp. 630, 633. (This is, incidentally, one of the most interesting
and penetrating discussions of Vaihinger's philosophy from the legal
standpoint.) The essentially technical character of the legal concept of
a "person" is well brought out in the chapter on "Personateness" in
Kocourek, *Jural Relations* (1927), p. 291.

tist. What I have called previously the fictions of emotional conservatism and of policy[67] and apologetic and merciful fictions[68] proceed from stresses in the judicial mind which, although probably not wholly unknown to the scientist, are nevertheless not an important factor in his mental life. But as I have shown before, even these fictions of applied law may proceed in some cases from motives essentially like those that impel the scientist to resort to "fiction."[69]

Before leaving this subject it might be well to point out that it is not always easy to distinguish between the process of discovering the facts of social life (descriptive science), and the process of establishing rules for the government of society (normative science). Much of what appears to be strictly juristic and normative is in fact an expression, not of a rule for the conduct of human beings, but of an opinion concerning the structure of society. Before one can intelligently determine what *should* be, one must determine what *is*, and in practice the two processes are often inseparably fused.

Probably the most violent critic of the law would not pretend that courts have ever been wholly oblivious to the social life in which their rules are to operate. Indeed, the courts were compelled to investigate the successions and interrelations of social life long before the disciplines of sociology, economics, psychology, political science, and anthropology were pursued as separate studies.

Jurisprudence was the first of the social sciences to be born. Of all men, judges and legislators were the first that found themselves compelled to seek a clear and conscious

---

[67] *Supra*, pp. 57–59.
[68] *Supra*, pp. 83–85.
[69] See the discussion of "intellectual conservatism," *supra*, pp. 63–70, and the heading "The Historical Legal Fiction Compared with Scientific Fictions," *supra*, pp. 71–72.

knowledge of the principles according to which human
beings live together.... Thus the law began to examine,
long before any later and independent sciences, created by
purely theoretical interests, took up the study of such matters, a large number of phenomena: logical and psychological ones, such as will, purpose, intention, declaration,
error, coercion, passion; economic ones, like estate, value,
price, utility; linguistic ones, like sentences, meanings;
ethical phenomena, such as liberty, personality, honesty;
political ones, like order, public authority, etc.[70]

Some legal fictions—far from being merely the metaphorical expressions of "norms"— are in fact expressions of scientific truths discovered by the courts in their struggle to rationalize the subject matters presented to them. For example,
the courts are frequently criticized for attributing legal consequences to an "intent" of the parties that is fictitious. This
"intent" is regarded as fictitious because it is not shown to
have been "present to the mind of the party." But is it not
possible that this "fictitious" intent represents the discovery
of an important psychological truth, namely, that the conduct of an individual may be accompanied and conditioned
by expectations that are not consciously present to his mind?

It should be recalled that the courts were pioneers not only
in the field of the social sciences, but perhaps in the field of
science generally. If we define science as the conscious generalization of experience, then the law was the first of the
sciences. In the words of Ihering,

> I believe it is not too much to say that it was in the field
> of the law that the human mind was first compelled to
> mount to abstraction; the first rule of law, whatever it may
> have concerned, was the first onset of the mind to con-
> scious generality of thought, the first occasion and the first
> attempt to lift itself above the sensuously obvious.[71]

[70] Wurzel, "Juridical Thinking" in *The Science of Legal Method*
(1917), pp. 286, 289, 291.
[71] *Geist des römischen Rechts auf den verschiedenen Stufen seiner
Entwicklung* (6th ed., 1923), II², 423.

That a whole host of juristic concepts have found useful application elsewhere is evidence enough that the ends of the law are not entirely peculiar to that science.[72] In this connection it is worth observing that the word "average," a word that stands for an important concept of science, is a law word.[73] Likewise, one of the most abstract and general words we have, the word "thing," is a law word.

If in recent years the law has begun to make use of the researches of the physical and social sciences, it is only receiving the return—we may hope with interest—of a loan made long ago.

Changing the Facts to Fit the Theory

It might be expected that in closing our discussion of the legal fiction we should attempt a summary of the views that have been developed in the course of this rather lengthy study. But the reader who has followed the discussion thus far will perhaps be willing to forgive the omission of such a summary. The matter is not simple enough to permit reduction to a compact formula.

But it would not be advisable to omit all mention of one criticism of the legal fiction that is usually advanced, even by those who pretend to some philosophic insight, with an air of complete finality. I refer to the contention that the fiction consists in "changing the facts to fit the theory," where

[72] "Law held the hegemony in the field of learning when ethical and political and social science were formative as certainly as the natural sciences dominate our thinking today. As today we resort to figures of speech drawn from organic creation and summon biological analogies to our aid in all fundamental difficulties, so men formerly resorted to juristic figures of speech and sought for legal analogies." Pound, "Legal Rights," 26 Int. Jour. of Ethics (1915), 92.

[73] "The sense of the word *average* has been generalized from a use connected with dividing loss by shipwreck proportionately among various sharers in an enterprise." Dewey, *How We Think* (1910), p. 183. The exact derivation of the word is disputed, but there seems to be no dispute that it was originally a law word.

the proper procedure is supposed to be "to change the theory
to fit the facts."[74] This criticism, sound as it may seem on its
face, is, philosophically considered, superficial. There is no
such thing as a plain, brute "fact," to which our theories ought
to conform.[75] All of our facts, at least all communicable facts
—those facts that go to make up what one writer has called
the "collective perception" of society[76]—are conceptual facts.
Our experiences, from earliest infancy on, are organized and
conceptualized by conventions of speech and thought. Our
language, our "common sense" notions, our scientific theories, our legal constructs—all of these are conceptual devices
for dealing with and organizing reality. "Facts" are only
those thought-constructs that are useful for so many purposes
and are so commonly accepted that no one doubts their "existence" or "reality." "Theories"—on the other hand—are
thought-constructs possessing a more restricted utility.

According to the prevailing popular theory—a theory for
which popular philosophy is largely indebted to a famous
lawyer, Francis Bacon—facts are "out there" in nature and
absolutely rigid, while principles are somewhere "in the
mind" under our scalps and changeable at will. According
to this view scientific theories are made to fit pre-existing
facts somewhat as clothes are made to fit people. A single

---

[74] Köhler makes this criticism of the legal fiction, and adds with in-
dignation, "What would one say today of a scientist who, in order to
rescue the Aristotelian system, would discipline the results of exact re-
search and thus, by shuffling and throwing a veil over them, reconcile
them with his system?" "Zwei Studien über das sogenante Repräsen-
tationsrecht" in Gesammelte Abhandlungen aus dem gemeinen und
französischen Civilrecht (1883), p. 368.

[75] Professor Walter Wheeler Cook, in speaking of the requirement in
the code pleading system that the complaint state only the "facts"
founding the action, says, " 'The facts as they actually existed or occurred,' 'the dry, naked, actual facts'—these and these only are to be
stated. Can it be done? I think not; it has never been done and never
will be done, either by a pleader or by anyone else. Philosophically,
logically, it is an impossibility." "The Utility of Jurisprudence in the
Solution of Legal Problems" Lectures on Legal Topics (Assn. of the
Bar of the City of N.Y.) V (1928), 337, 369.

[76] Ajtay, Le chemin le plus court de la pensée juridique (n.d.), p. 38.

inconsistent fact, and the whole theory is abandoned. Actually, however, facts are not so rigid and theories not so flexible; and when the two do not fit, the process of adaptation is a bilateral one. When new facts come up inconsistent with previous theories, we do not give up the latter, but modify both the facts and the theory by the introduction of new distinctions or of hypothetical elements.[77]

All this is not to say that there is not usually underlying the criticism of the fiction mentioned a certain hard common sense. When we say that a fiction "changes the facts to fit the theory," what we usually mean is that in adjusting our conceptual apparatus to accommodate a new situation, we have made the adjustment in a clumsy way and in the wrong place. We should accomplish the change in the realm of those constructs which are already specialized (in the realm of "theory") rather than in the realm of those widely accepted and inclusive constructs which we call "facts." It is wiser, for example, to alter the juridical notion of the conditions under which trover may be maintained than it is to attempt to tamper with such a common concept as "finding."

Conclusion

It would perhaps be wise to issue a warning at the conclusion of this study against an inference that might be made from the account of Vaihinger's philosophy which has been given on these pages. In these days when so much is said against "conceptualism" one might be tempted to rely upon the philosophy of "As If" as support for the thesis that intellectual concepts generally are a bad thing, and that we ought to lose no time in ridding the law of everything that savors of generalization. Nothing could be more foreign to Vaihinger.

[77] Cohen, "The Place of Logic in the Law," 29 *Harv. L. Rev.* (1916), 622, 626. Similar ideas are expressed in Demogue, *Les notions fondamentales du droit privé* (1911), p. 249, and Ajtay, *ibid.*, p. 38. See also Polanyi, *The Logic of Liberty* (1951) and *Personal Knowledge* (1958); and Kuhn, *The Structure of Scientific Revolutions* (1962).

Vaihinger is not opposed to conceptualism, but only to clumsy, hypostatizing conceptualism. He recognizes that concepts form the very substance of thought, and that without the many "fictions" which he enumerates thinking would be impossible.

So many tirades have been launched against "conceptualism" that one sometimes gains the impression that certain writers expect us to accomplish the impossible feat of reasoning without concepts. The trouble with the law does not lie in its use of concepts, nor even in its use of "lump concepts." The difficulty lies in part in the fact that we have sometimes put the "lumps" in the wrong places, and in part in the fact that we have often forgotten that the "lumps" are the creations of our own minds.

No theory or dogma can solve the problem of how far we ought to generalize or "conceptualize" the law. It is a question of balance and judgment. In this connection certain words written in 1781 may not be without significance:

> This distinction shows itself in the different manner of thought among students of nature, some of them (who are pre-eminently speculative) being almost averse to heterogeneousness, and always intent on the unity of genera; while others, pre-eminently empirical, are constantly striving to divide nature into so much variety that one might lose almost all hope of being able to judge its phenomena according to general principles ... In this manner one philosopher is influenced more by the interest of *diversity* (according to the principle of specification), another by the interests of *unity* (according to the principle of aggregation). *Each believes that he has derived his judgment from his insight into the object, and yet founds it entirely on the greater or smaller attachment to one of the two principles, neither of which rests on objective grounds, but only on an interest of reason.*[78]

[78] Kant, *The Critique of Pure Reason* (Müller's transl., 1881), pp. 561–62, 571–72. (Italics of last sentence are mine.)

The ultimate problem of the law is balance. Nothing will take the place, in a student of the law, of a sense of tact and balance—not even a burning desire to "get the facts" or to know the "societal background." Is it mere accident that it is a law word, the word "judgment," which has come in common speech to express precisely this sense of tact and balance, so indispensable in any abstract science?

Index